BELIEFS,
ATTITUDES,
AND HUMAN AFFAIRS

BASIC CONCEPTS IN PSYCHOLOGY SERIES

Edward L. Walker, Editor

GENERAL

PSYCHOLOGY AS A NATURAL AND SOCIAL SCIENCE	Edward L. Walker
TEACHING THE BEGINNING COURSE IN PSYCHOLOGY	Edward L. Walker and Wilbert J. McKeachie
A LABORATORY MANUAL FOR THE CONTROL AND ANALYSIS OF BEHAVIOR	Harlan L. Lane and Daryl J. Bem
QUANTIFICATION IN PSYCHOLOGY	William L. Hays
BASIC STATISTICS	William L. Hays

PSYCHOLOGY: A NATURAL SCIENCE

NEUROPSYCHOLOGY: THE STUDY OF BRAIN AND BEHAVIOR	Charles M. Butter
SENSORY PROCESSES	Mathew Alpern, Merle Lawrence, and David Wolsk
PERCEPTION	Daniel J. Weintraub and Edward L. Walker
PERCEPTUAL DEMONSTRATION KIT	Daniel J. Weintraub and Edward L. Walker
HUMAN PERFORMANCE	Paul M. Fitts and Michael I. Posner
CONDITIONING AND INSTRUMENTAL LEARNING	Edward L. Walker
COMPARATIVE PSYCHOLOGY	Richard A. Maier and Barbara M. Maier

PSYCHOLOGY: A SOCIAL SCIENCE

MOTIVATION: A STUDY OF ACTION	David Birch and Joseph Veroff
THE CONCEPT OF HUMAN DEVELOPMENT	Elton B. McNeil
PSYCHODYNAMICS: THE SCIENCE OF UNCONSCIOUS MENTAL FORCES	Gerald S. Blum
ASSESSMENT OF HUMAN CHARACTERISTICS	E. Lowell Kelly
COGNITIVE PROCESSES	Melvin Manis
SOCIAL PSYCHOLOGY: AN EXPERIMENTAL APPROACH	Robert B. Zajonc
NON-FREUDIAN PERSONALITY THEORIES	P. James Geiwitz
BELIEFS, ATTITUDES, AND HUMAN AFFAIRS	Daryl J. Bem
CLINICAL PSYCHOLOGY: AN EMPIRICAL APPROACH	Erasmus L. Hoch
ABNORMAL PSYCHOLOGY	James Neal Butcher

BELIEFS,
ATTITUDES,
AND HUMAN AFFAIRS

DARYL J. BEM

Cornell University

BROOKS/COLE PUBLISHING COMPANY
Monterey, California

A Division of Wadsworth, Inc.

To

Reed College, my first mistress,

and Sandy, my current one

15   14   13

ISBN 0-8185-8906-X

L.C. Cat. Card No. 71-95057

Printed in the United States of America

SERIES FOREWORD

Basic Concepts in Psychology was conceived as a series of brief paperback volumes constituting a beginning textbook in psychology. Several unique advantages arise from publishing individual chapters as separate volumes rather than under a single cover. Each book or chapter can be written by an author identified with the subject matter of the area. New chapters can be added, individual chapters can be revised independently, and, possibly, competitive chapters can be provided for controversial areas. Finally, to a degree, an instructor of the beginning course in psychology can choose a particular set of chapters to meet the needs of his students.

Probably the most important impetus for the series came from the fact that a suitable textbook did not exist for the beginning courses in psychology at the University of Michigan—Psychology 100 (Psychology as a Natural Science) and Psychology 101 (Psychology as a Social Science). In addition, no laboratory manual treated both the natural science and social science problems encountered in the first laboratory course, Psychology 110.

For practical rather than ideological reasons most of the original complement of authors came from the staff of the University of Michigan. As the series has developed, authors have been selected from other institutions in an effort to assure national representation and a broad perspective in contemporary psychology.

Each author in the Basic Concepts in Psychology Series has considerable freedom. He has been charged to devote approximately half of his resources to elementary concepts and half to topics of special interest and emphasis. In this way, each volume will reflect the personality and viewpoint of the author while presenting the subject matter usually found in a chapter of an elementary textbook.

PREFACE

Beliefs and attitudes play an important role in human affairs. And when public policy is being formulated, beliefs *about* beliefs and attitudes probably play an even more crucial role. Accordingly, the United States Supreme Court, congressional committees, presidential commissions, and other public decision-making bodies have turned increasingly to behavioral scientists for information and, occasionally, advice concerning the how, what, and why of men's beliefs and attitudes. This book is written for any citizen who wants to understand some of the conceptual and empirical knowledge behind that information and advice. It is an essay on the psychological foundations of beliefs and attitudes.

The theoretical discussion itself is reasonably comprehensive, eclectic, noncontroversial, and apolitical. But the examples are not. They are deliberately chosen to illustrate how personal and political considerations become not only relevant but unavoidable when the scientist travels from his conceptual and empirical knowledge to his advice, when he travels from the campus to the Capitol. Certainly not all behavioral scientists, nor even all social psychologists, share the political coloration that emerges from my personal selection of examples (although evidence discussed in Chapter 4 reveals that I am not atypical). The important point I have tried to convey, however, is that political coloration of some sort is always added during the trip to Washington. Citizens and public decision-makers ought, in my view, to know that, too.

Thus, the extended examples in this book make it unmistakably a personal essay. Unlike most examples in textbooks, those here are more than "pedagogical aids to understanding." They are the chocolate chips which give the cookie its flavor and, let us hope, make it worth the eating.

I am grateful for the assistance of several people who commented upon earlier drafts of the manuscript: Barry F. Anderson of Portland State College; Theodore M. Newcomb and Edward L. Walker, both of the University of Michigan; and Eve V. Clark, Herbert H. Clark, and Philip G. Zimbardo, all of Stanford University.

The influence of Thomas F. Pettigrew is more pervasive than the explicit citations to his published work indicate. It was his Harvard course in race relations which prompted me to terminate my graduate work in physics and initiate my career in psychology. It was he who first demonstrated to me the relevance of social psychological research to human affairs. Many sections of this book contain his examples; all attempt to follow his example.

Dr. Sandra L. Bem, research psychologist and faculty member at Leland Stanford University, not only made suggestions throughout the book but joined with me in the writing of its final section, "Case Study of a Nonconscious Ideology: Training the Woman to Know Her Place." There it becomes apparent why she did not type the manuscript, prepare the index, keep children out of my hair, display spectacular indulgence and patience during the writing of this book, nor do any of those other things for which wives traditionally earn affectionate footnotes.* There, too, it becomes apparent why she is my best friend, my colleague, and my lover. Without her companionship, this book undoubtedly would have been finished several months earlier.

---

*An affectionate footnote is in order, however, for Charles T. Hendrix of Brooks/Cole, who did display spectacular indulgence and patience during the writing of this book, and for my mother-in-law, Lillian L. Lipsitz, who did type the manuscript.

CONTENTS

BELIEFS,
ATTITUDES,
AND HUMAN AFFAIRS

INTRODUCTION AND OVERVIEW: THE PSYCHOLOGICAL FOUNDATIONS OF BELIEFS AND ATTITUDES

In 1896 the United States Supreme Court gave judicial sanction to the "separate but equal" doctrine of race relations by ruling that legalized racial segregation did not violate the Constitution. In 1954 the Court reversed this earlier decision when it declared legalized racial segregation in the public schools to be inherently unequal and, hence, a violation of Constitutional rights. In reaching this conclusion, the 1954 Court considered a number of social science documents, which it cited in a footnote to the decision.

Opponents of the 1954 decision quickly seized upon this fact and expressed their dismay that the Court had strayed from its obligation to render purely legal decisions and had contaminated its deliberations with psychological and sociological considerations. As the editor of the *Richmond Times-Dispatch* in Virginia put it, "The violence at Little Rock . . . never would have happened if nine justices had not consulted sociologists and psychologists, instead of lawyers, in 1954, and attempted to legislate through judicial decrees" (Dabney, 1957, p. 14; quoted by Pettigrew, 1961).

Such critics clearly favored the "purely legal" decision of 1896, in which the Court explicitly recognized that "legislation is powerless to eradicate racial instincts," and upheld the view that "stateways cannot change folkways."

But this criticism of the 1954 decision carries its own refutation by revealing that the 1896 decision was equally as "sociological and psychological." Thus, the notion that there are "racial instincts" and the belief that legislative or judicial action does not produce attitude change are psychological assumptions which require empirical evidence for or against them. They are neither self-evident truths nor historic legal principles. In fact, even the language used by the 1896 Court in justifying its decision reads as if it were lifted directly from the writings of William Graham Sumner, the influential sociologist of the day who maintained that "stateways cannot change folkways."

Thus, if there is a significant difference between the 1896 and 1954 decisions, it resides not in the legal purity of their reasonings but in the difference between nineteenth and twentieth century knowledge about beliefs and attitudes. The 1896 Court was simply less scholarly than the 1954 Court in acknowledging its sociological and psychological sources explicitly. As we shall see in the final two chapters of this book, we now believe that stateways can, indeed, change folkways.

But it is the moral of this example I wish to emphasize here: Legislation and court decisions are *always* influenced by sociological and psychological assumptions. Our entire legal system has such assumptions buried within it. Beliefs concerning the conditions under which a man can be held to be freely responsible for his acts, assumptions about the ability of capital punishment to deter crime, and questions of what is òr is not obscene—all involve psychological assumptions. Those in decision-making positions cannot avoid them; they can only deal with them knowingly and explicitly, as the 1954 Court did, or unwittingly allow them to enter through the back door, as the 1896 Court did. Beliefs *about* beliefs and attitudes play a crucial role in the formulation of public policy. And, since America is ideologically committed to having its citizens participate in the decision-making process as much as possible, I should like those citizens to base their decisions upon twentieth century beliefs about beliefs and attitudes. Furthermore, I should like them to do so knowingly rather than unwittingly. These are the considerations which motivated the writing of this book and largely determined its content.

A man's beliefs and attitudes have their foundations in four human activities: thinking, feeling, behaving, and interacting with others. Accordingly, this book divides the psychological foundations of beliefs and attitudes into four parts: *cognitive foundations, emotional foundations, behavioral foundations,* and *social foundations.*

Chapters 2, 3, and 4 deal with the cognitive foundations, exploring the logic, or "psycho-logic,"[1] that ties a man's opinions together. How are his beliefs, attitudes, and values interrelated? What are the conscious, nonconscious, and unconscious components of his thinking? Is a man consistent or inconsistent in his opinions?

In answering such questions, these three chapters discuss stereotypes, the "new politics," anti-Semitism, the relationships between Christian beliefs and racial prejudice, the political beliefs of behavioral scientists, and American liberalism and conservatism.

Chapter 5, on emotional foundations, discusses the underlying processes by which our feelings, the emotional components of beliefs and attitudes, are acquired, transmitted, modified, and eliminated. This chapter also asks the deceptively simple question "How do we know what we are feeling?"

Examples in Chapter 5 include a brief look at the lie detector,

---

[1]My use of the term "psycho-logic" is broader and looser than Abelson and Rosenberg's (1958).

the origin of emotional reactions to racial terms and "dirty" words, the effects of violence and nudity in the mass media, a theory about why obese Jews can fast more easily than Jews of normal weight—but only if they go to the synagogue—and a novel way to get more enjoyment out of your *Playboy* centerfold.

Chapter 6, on the behavioral foundations of beliefs and attitudes, challenges the common assumption that one cannot change the behavior of men until one has changed their "hearts and minds" first. Two theories are examined which imply that, in fact, one of the most effective ways of changing the "hearts and minds" of men is to change their behavior first. Chapter 6 also explores the conditions under which "saying becomes believing," and presents the testimony I gave before a Senate subcommittee on the possible psychological effects of police interrogation upon the memory of a suspect.

The seventh and final chapter of the book, on social foundations, surveys the many social influences that create and modify men's beliefs, attitudes, and values. The chapter begins with a discussion of the most superficial form of social influence, persuasion via the mass media; it then progresses through the more profound forms of influence that family, friends, teachers, and colleagues have on our belief systems, and ends with a discussion of society's ability to inculcate an entire ideology into its citizens. This discussion of social influences also tries to puncture some of the claims for aspirin which emanate from our television screens, takes a look at the social norms behind the desegregation process, and presents a biased view of the generation gap. The book ends with a lengthy dissertation on the role of woman in our society and on the hidden ideology which so effectively "keeps her in her place."

Certain opinions seem to go together. For example: I support strong civil rights legislation; I was always a "dove" on Vietnam; I am more afraid of fascism than of communism in our country; I worry less about the size of our national debt than about the unequal distribution of our national wealth; I believe that college women should no more be subjected to curfews than college men; and I think the Black Power movement is a good thing. On their surface, these diverse opinions do not seem to follow logically from one another—there are even some implied inconsistencies among them—and yet, if you knew only one of my opinions, you could probably guess the others with pretty fair accuracy. Certain opinions do seem to go together.

Of course, there does seem to be a kind of logic involved here. The opinions given above all appear to follow more or less from a common set of underlying values (such as equality, for example). This can be true of "conservative" opinions as well. For example, my neighbor says that his major value is individual freedom and that therefore he is opposed to open-housing laws and to legislation which regulates the possession of firearms. I may disagree with his opinions, but I can appreciate the logic involved. Curiously, however, my freedom-loving neighbor also advocates stiffer penalties for the use of marijuana, feels that women belong in the home, and believes that consenting adults who engage in homosexual behavior should get long prison terms. Here the logic involved is less than clear, yet these opinions too seem strangely predictable. Indeed, my neighbor and I both profess to hold individual freedom as a basic value, and we both claim that our opinions are consistent with our values. Yet we find each other's opinions highly disagreeable.

In short, beliefs, attitudes, and values do seem to be logically connected, but in some instances the logic seems more Freudian than Aristotelian. It is this mixture of logic and psycho-logic that concerns us in this and the following two chapters. It is this mixture of logic and psycho-logic that constitutes the cognitive foundations of beliefs and attitudes.

PRIMITIVE BELIEFS

If a man perceives some relationship between two things or between some thing and a characteristic of it, he is said to hold a belief. For example, he might suppose asteroids and oranges to be round, the dean of women to be square, God to be dead, men to love freedom, himself to dislike spinach, and Republicans to promote progress. Collectively, a man's beliefs compose his understanding of himself and his environment.

Many beliefs are the product of direct experience. If you ask your friends why they believe oranges are round, they will most likely reply that they have seen oranges, felt oranges, and that oranges are, indeed, round. And that would seem to end the matter. You could, of course, ask them why they trust their senses, but that would be impolite.

Consider a more complicated belief. If you ask your friends why they believe the asteroids are round (that is, spherical), the more sophisticated among them might be able to show how such a conclusion is derived from physical principles and astronomical observations. You could press them further by asking them to justify their belief in physical principles and astronomical observations: Whence comes their knowledge of such things? When they answer that question—perhaps by citing the *New York Times*—you can continue to probe: Why do they believe everything they read in the *Times?* If they then refer to previous experience with the accuracy of the *Times* or recall that their teachers always had kind words for its journalistic integrity, challenge the validity of their previous experience or the credibility of their teachers.

What you will discover by such questioning—besides a noticeable decline in the number of your friends—is that every belief can be pushed back until it is seen to rest ultimately upon a basic belief in the credibility of one's own sensory experience or upon a basic belief in the credibility of some external authority. Other beliefs may derive from these basic beliefs, but the basic beliefs themselves are accepted as givens. Accordingly, we shall call them "primitive beliefs."[1]

ZERO-ORDER BELIEFS

Our most fundamental primitive beliefs are so taken for granted that we are apt not to notice that we hold them at all; we remain unaware of them until they are called to our attention or are brought into question by some bizarre circumstance in which they appear to be violated. For example, we believe that an object continues to exist even when we are not looking at it; we believe that objects remain the same size and shape as we move away from them even though their visual images change; and, more generally, we believe that our perceptual and conceptual worlds have a degree of orderliness and stability over time. Our faith in the validity of our sensory experience is the most important primitive belief of all.

[1] I have borrowed and slightly modified the concept of a primitive belief from Rokeach (1968).

These are among the first beliefs that a child learns as he interacts with his environment, and in a psychological sense, they are continuously validated by experience. As a result, we are usually unaware of the fact that alternatives to these beliefs *could* exist, and it is precisely for this reason that we remain unaware of the beliefs themselves. Only a very unparochial and intellectual fish is aware that his environment is wet. What else could it be? We shall call primitive beliefs of this fundamental kind "zero-order" beliefs. They are the "nonconscious" axioms upon which our other beliefs are built.[2]

FIRST-ORDER BELIEFS

Because we implicitly hold these zero-order beliefs about the trustworthiness of our senses, particular beliefs that are based upon direct sensory experiences seem to carry their own justification. When a man justifies his belief in the roundness of oranges by citing his experiences with oranges, that in fact usually does end the matter. He does not run through a syllogistic argument of the form:

> 1st Premise: My senses tell me that oranges are round.
> 2nd Premise: My senses tell me true.
> Conclusion: Therefore, oranges are round.

There is no such inferential process involved in going from the first premise to the conclusion, as far as the individual himself is concerned, because he takes the second premise for granted: it is a zero-order belief. Accordingly, the first premise ("My senses tell me that oranges are round") is psychologically synonymous with the conclusion ("Oranges are round"). We shall call such conclusions "first-order" beliefs. Unlike zero-order beliefs, an individual is usually aware of his first-order beliefs because he can readily imagine alternatives to them (oranges could be square), but he is usually *not* aware of any inferential process by which they derive from zero-order beliefs. Like zero-order beliefs, then, first-order beliefs are still appropriately called primitive beliefs—that is, beliefs which demand no independent formal or empirical confirmation and which require no justification beyond a brief citation of direct experience.

PRIMITIVE BELIEFS BASED ON EXTERNAL AUTHORITY

We not only experience our world directly, we are told about it as well. It is in this way that notions about such intangibles as God, absent

---

[2] I have chosen the word "nonconscious" to characterize the kind of unawareness described here. In this book, the term "unconscious" is reserved for beliefs or attitudes that we "repress" or keep out of awareness because we find them too painful to admit to ourselves. We shall see examples in the next chapter.

grandmothers, and threatened tooth decay first enter a child's system of beliefs. And to the child, such beliefs may seem as direct, as palpable, and as assuredly valid as any beliefs based on direct sensory encounter. When mommy says that not brushing after every meal causes tooth decay, that is synonymous with the *fact* that not brushing after every meal causes tooth decay. Such a belief is a primitive first-order belief for the child because the intervening premise, "Mommy says only true things," is nonconscious; the possibility that mommy sometimes says false things is not a conceivable alternative. First-order beliefs based upon a zero-order belief in the credibility of an external authority, then, are functionally no different from first-order beliefs based upon an axiomatic belief in the credibility of our senses. As sources of information, mommy and our senses are equally reliable. Our implicit faiths in them are zero-order beliefs.

This emphasis upon the innocence of childhood should not obscure the fact that we all hold primitive beliefs. It is an epistemological and psychological necessity, not a flaw of intellect or a surplus of naïveté. We all share the fundamental zero-order beliefs about our senses, and most of us hold similar sorts of first-order beliefs. For example, we rarely question beliefs such as "This woman is my mother" and "I am a human being." Most of us even treat arbitrary social-linguistic conventions like "This is my left hand" and "Today is Tuesday" as if they were physical bits of knowledge handed down by some authority who "really knows." Finally, most religious and quasi-religious beliefs are first-order beliefs based upon an unquestioned zero-order faith in some internal or external source of knowledge. The child who sings "Jesus loves me—this I know, / For the Bible tells me so" is actually being less evasive about the metaphysical—and hence nonconfirmable—nature of his belief than our founding fathers were when they presumed to interpret reality for King George III: "We hold these truths to be self-evident . . ."

GENERALIZATIONS AND STEREOTYPES

Very few of our primitive beliefs rest directly upon a single experience. Most of them are abstractions or generalizations from several experiences over time. Thus an individual may believe life in the city to be hectic, John to be generous, freedom to be wonderful, and modern art to be hard to understand. Each such belief arises out of several separate situations, but because the individual still relates such beliefs to direct experience, they are properly classified as primitive beliefs. As far as the individual is concerned, they still spring directly from a source whose credibility is axiomatic and self-evident: his senses.

But life in the city is not always hectic; John has been stingy on occasion; freedom is sometimes not so wonderful; and modern art is frequently comprehensible. Generalizations, in short, are not always true for all instances beyond the set of experiences upon which they are based. And when an individual treats such generalizations as if they were universally true, we usually call them stereotypes. For a number of reasons, most of us have learned to regard stereotypes as undesirable. Sometimes, for example, stereotypes are based upon no valid experience at all but are picked up as hearsay or are formed to rationalize our prejudices. Then, too, stereotypes are frequently used to justify shabby treatment of individuals on the basis of assumed group characteristics which neither they nor the group, in fact, possess.

But it is important to realize that the process by which most stereotypes arise is not itself evil or pathological. Generalizing from a limited set of experiences and treating individuals as members of a group are not only common cognitive acts but necessary ones. They are "thinking devices" which enable us to avoid conceptual chaos by "packaging" our world into a manageable number of categories. It is simply not possible to deal with every situation or person as if it or he were unique, and the formation of "working stereotypes" is inevitable until further experiences either refine or discredit them. For example, many freshmen from rural areas of the country spend the first few weeks of college thinking all New Yorkers are Jews and all Jews are New Yorkers. There is not necessarily any malice or ill will behind such a stereotype; the freshman has simply not yet seen the distinguishing characteristics of Jews and New Yorkers uncorrelated—if there are such characteristics. But when his "obviously-New-York-Jewish" roommate turns out to be a Christian Scientist from New Jersey named Murphy, and the Texan with cowboy boots allows as how his father is a rabbi in Houston, the freshman soon begins to sort his social environment into more finely differentiated categories. I suspect that most of our stereotypes are of this benign variety and that we learn to discard the irrelevant characteristics from our social categories as our experiences broaden and multiply.

The most important word here, however, is "broaden." The new experiences must be the kind which does, in fact, separate the relevant characteristics from the irrelevant ones, not the kind which serves to reinforce the stereotypes. For example, it is often suggested that increased contact between ethnic groups will automatically cause the disappearance of stereotypes. But nobody has more interracial contact than black ghetto residents and white policemen. Yet these interracial contacts are not particularly noted for producing spectacular interracial tolerance. The point, of course, is that the white policemen deal primarily with the criminal element within the ghetto and that the black residents see precisely those whites in the ghetto who are cast in authoritarian roles. Such contacts only reinforce the stereotypes on both sides because the racial identification continues to be coupled with the irrelevant characteristics.

The worst failure of such contacts is not that they occur in hostile situations (although that certainly doesn't help) but that the participants are not of equal status (Allport, 1954). Thus, we see similar kinds of stereotypes being maintained on both sides even in the more benign encounters between black ghetto residents and white shop owners or welfare agency employees, where, again, the equal-status requirement is not fulfilled. It is when this requirement is satisfied that the participants are most likely to see each other as sharing common beliefs, attributes, and goals, rather than perceiving each other as participants in the old stereotyped roles.

The kind of vicarious interracial contact supplied by the mass media must operate on this same principle of equal-status representation if it too is to be helpful in eliminating stereotypes. In 1968, after years of pressure from civil rights organizations, the mass media finally began to observe this principle by regularly featuring black faces in other than "Negro" roles. Thus, although television commercials may continue to offend our sensibilities for other reasons, they actually do help Americans lose their stereotypes—if only by demonstrating that any odors black Americans may have are the familiar kinds which can be cured by Dial or Listerine.

But if some stereotypes are vulnerable to new experiences, many others can be remarkably impervious to evidence against them. Even repeated disconfirmations of a stereotype can often fail to alter it because the individual treats them as exceptions. Thus, he notes that there is Sidney Poitier or Supreme Court Justice Thurgood Marshall—but then there are "all the rest of them." And some stereotypes are even more cleverly insulated from reality than this because the individual sees to it that there is no way even for exceptions to occur. He simply never bothers to check the stereotype against an independent criterion. For instance, many people claim they can "spot a homosexual a mile away." They can do no such thing, of course. What they can do is recognize a man who displays slightly effeminate gestures, and when they do, they proclaim that they have "spotted another homosexual," thereby reinforcing their stereotype. But since they decline to ascertain the sexual preferences of the "spotted" individual, their reasoning is purely circular. They thus mistakenly classify as homosexual large numbers of nonhomosexual individuals who display effeminate gestures. The man who lays claim to such "homosexual radar" might be mildly unhappy to learn that he is misclassifying these individuals, but it is a safe bet that he would be considerably more agitated to learn that he is failing to detect all those homosexuals who are so inconsiderate as to mingle in our midst without an identifying "swish." But he is safe: since evidence plays no valid role in the maintenance of such a stereotype, it is effectively insulated against either kind of disconfirmation, and he will never know.

Stereotypes, then, are overgeneralized beliefs based on too limited a set of experiences. Whether stereotypes are evil or benign in their consequences, they are like other first-order primitive beliefs in that they appear to the individual to be self-evident; they appear to demand no justification beyond a citation either of direct experience or of some external authority whose credibility is taken for granted, whose credibility, in other words, is a zero-order primitive belief. All of us rely upon stereotypes to some extent for "packaging" our perceptual and conceptual worlds.

HIGHER-ORDER BELIEFS

THE VERTICAL STRUCTURE OF BELIEFS

Although we all hold primitive beliefs throughout our lives, we learn as we leave childhood behind us to regard our sensory experiences as potentially fallible and similarly learn to be more cautious in believing external authorities. We begin, in short, to insert an explicit and conscious premise about an authority's credibility between his word and our belief:[3]

> The Surgeon General says that smoking causes cancer.
> The Surgeon General is a trustworthy expert.
> Therefore, smoking causes cancer.

In such cases, we no longer treat the first premise as synonymous with the conclusion because the second premise is no longer a nonconscious zero-order belief. We are, for example, explicitly aware of the possibility that the Surgeon General might be in error. Accordingly, the conclusion "Smoking causes cancer" is not a primitive belief but rather a derived, or higher-order, belief. It has a "vertical structure" of beliefs underneath it, beliefs which "generate" it as the product of quasi-logical inference.

We also learn to derive higher-order beliefs by reasoning inductively from our experiences:

> My aunt contracted cancer.
> She died soon after.
> Therefore, cancer can cause death.

---

[3] I have borrowed the idea of using syllogisms to characterize beliefs and attitudes from Jones and Gerard (1967). They are not, of course, responsible for the modifications I have introduced.

And finally, we can derive beliefs of a still higher order by building upon premises which are themselves conclusions of prior syllogisms. For example, we can use as premises the conclusions to the two syllogisms above:

> Smoking causes cancer.
> Cancer can cause death.
> Therefore, smokers die younger than nonsmokers.

Note that it is possible for two men to hold the same surface belief but to have different vertical structures of belief. For example, the Surgeon General believes that smokers die younger on the average than nonsmokers, but so also does the man who believes that:

> Smoking is a sin.
> The wages of sin is death.
> Therefore, smokers die younger than nonsmokers.

But the Surgeon General's belief is a higher-order belief based upon a long chain of careful syllogistic reasoning, whereas, for this man, the same conclusion, or surface belief, is only a second-order belief (based on two first-order primitive beliefs).

When a belief has a deep vertical structure, it is said to be highly elaborated or differentiated; to the extent that it has little or no syllogistic reasoning underneath it, it is said to be unelaborated or undifferentiated. A primitive belief is, by definition, completely undifferentiated.

THE HORIZONTAL STRUCTURE OF BELIEFS

We might expect higher-order beliefs to be quite vulnerable to disconfirmation because any one of the underlying premises could be destroyed. Thus, a higher-order belief would appear to be only as strong as its weakest link. This would be true if most higher-order beliefs were not also bolstered by "horizontal" structures as well. That is, a particular higher-order belief is often the conclusion to more than one syllogistic chain of reasoning. For example, the Surgeon General believes that:

Smoking causes cancer.	Smokers drink more heavily than nonsmokers.	Statistics show smokers die younger than nonsmokers.
Cancer can cause death.	Heavy drinking can lead to early death.	These statistics are reliable.
Therefore, smokers die younger.	Therefore, smokers die younger.	Therefore, smokers die younger.

If a man derives his belief that "smokers die younger" from all three lines of reasoning, then his belief will only be partially weakened if one of the syllogisms is faulty or one of the premises turns out to be false. It seems likely that most of our higher-order beliefs rest not upon a single syllogistic pillar but upon many. They have broad horizontal as well as deep vertical structures.

In the course of time, the vertical and horizontal structures of a higher-order belief can change without disturbing the belief itself. We believe as we did before, but our reasons for believing have altered. For example, all the evidence upon which we once based our trust in the *New York Times* may have faded from memory until now our devotion is a blind article of faith, a zero-order belief. Alternatively, additional support may have been obtained for beliefs that were once primitive beliefs or otherwise lacking in respectable justification.

THE CENTRALITY OF BELIEFS

A belief which has both a broad horizontal and a deep vertical structure is still not necessarily a very important or central belief in an individual's belief system. For example, my belief that asteroids are spherical is based on several different kinds of evidence, and some of the chains of reasoning behind the belief are quite lengthy. My belief therefore has a broad horizontal and a deep vertical structure; it is broadly based and highly differentiated. But if my belief in round asteroids were to be changed somehow, few of my other beliefs would have to be changed as a consequence. In terms of our syllogistic model, many syllogisms lead up to my belief in round asteroids, but few syllogisms depart from it; it appears as a conclusion to many syllogisms but enters as a premise into very few. This is what is meant by saying that the belief is not very central in my belief system.

Highly differentiated and broadly based beliefs are not necessarily central; the opposite is also true. For example, primitive beliefs are, by definition, completely undifferentiated; they have neither vertical nor horizontal support. And yet many of our primitive beliefs are very central in our belief systems. In fact, our primitive zero-order belief in the general credibility of our senses is the most central belief of all; nearly all of our other beliefs rest upon it, and to lose our faith in it is to lose our sanity. Also, as noted earlier, most of our religious and philosophical beliefs are primitive first-order beliefs upon which many of our other beliefs are built. They, too, are central.

Beliefs, then, differ from one another in the degree to which they are differentiated (vertical structure), in the extent to which they are broadly based (horizontal structure), and in their underlying importance to other beliefs (centrality). These are some of the major factors that contribute to the complexity and richness of our cognitive belief systems.

LOGIC VERSUS PSYCHO-LOGIC

Underlying the syllogistic description of beliefs presented in this chapter is the notion that individuals do not merely subscribe to random collections of beliefs but rather they maintain coherent systems of beliefs which are internally consistent. This central theme has been the basis for a number of recent psychological theories, called "cognitive consistency" theories, which we shall examine in detail in Chapter 4. But it is appropriate to point out here that to say that a man is consistent is not necessarily to say that he is logical or rational. Thus, even though we have employed the syllogism as a convenient way of representing the structure of beliefs, many of the examples have shown that we are not dealing with strict deductive logic but rather with a kind of psycho-logic. First of all, an inductive generalization based upon experience is often faulty—as our discussion of stereotypes has indicated. Second, even when the logic itself is impeccably deductive, the conclusions to syllogisms can be wrong if any one of the underlying premises is false. Third, there are often inconsistencies between different higher-order beliefs even though the internal reasoning behind each separate belief is consistent within its own vertical structure. That is, one line of reasoning leads to one conclusion; a second line leads to a contradictory conclusion. Finally, as we shall see in Chapter 4, one's attitudes and "ulterior motives" can distort the reasoning process so that the logic itself is subtly illogical. When I mention this final point in class, my students are quick to provide their parents' favorite syllogism as an example:

> Most heroin addicts started on marijuana.
> You kids are experimenting with marijuana.
> Therefore, you will become heroin addicts.

As my students suggest in rebuttal, most heroin addicts started on mother's milk. Therefore . . .

THE COGNITIVE FOUNDATIONS OF ATTITUDES

Attitudes are likes and dislikes. They are our affinities for and our aversions to situations, objects, persons, groups, or any other identifiable aspects of our environment, including abstract ideas and social policies. As we shall see in Chapters 5, 6, and 7, our likes and dislikes have roots in our emotions, in our behavior, and in the social influences upon us. But they also rest upon cognitive foundations. Attitudes, like beliefs, can be the conclusions to syllogisms.

EVALUATIVE BELIEFS

Most of us are indifferent to the shape of oranges; in pronouncing oranges round, we are not rendering a value judgment. But many of our beliefs *are* evaluative in nature: when we assert that the dean of women is square, we imply evaluation, not just description. Everything that has been said up to this point about beliefs in general also applies to evaluative beliefs in particular. For example, they can be primitive beliefs based upon a single sensory experience ("Spinach tastes terrible"), abstract primitive beliefs based upon several separate experiences ("Freedom is desirable"), or primitive beliefs based upon authority ("God is good"). Evaluative beliefs can also be higher-order beliefs. In particular, higher-order evaluative beliefs are derived from syllogisms in which a nonevaluative belief serves as the first premise and an evaluative belief serves as the second premise:

> Black economic power will bring about racial justice
> and equality.
> Racial justice and equality are desirable.
> Therefore, black economic power is desirable.

And, as in the case of beliefs generally, higher-order evaluative beliefs can enter into further syllogisms to yield evaluative beliefs of a still higher order:

> Black cooperatives will promote black economic power.
> Black economic power is desirable.
> Therefore, black cooperatives are desirable.

Evaluative beliefs are often referred to as the "cognitive component" of attitudes because they can serve as a partial basis for our likes and dislikes. For example, consider the following syllogism:

> Spinach has a terrible taste.
> I dislike terrible tastes.
> Therefore, I dislike spinach.

The first premise is an evaluative belief, and the conclusion is an attitude statement, an individual's statement about one of his own likes and dislikes. This syllogism appears trivial because we so often like things which we evaluate positively and dislike things which we evaluate negatively that we typically do not distinguish between an evaluative belief and an attitude that follows directly from it. The first premise and the conclusion are treated as synonymous because the middle premise is so frequently true that it has become a nonconscious belief. The middle premise is rarely acknowledged explicitly. "Terrible tastes" are disliked almost by definition.

But there are exceptions to this link between an evaluative belief and an attitude. For example, consider the following "nonsyllogism":

> Cigarettes taste terrible, cause cancer, make me cough, and offend others.
> I dislike terrible tastes, cancer, coughing, and offending others.
> But I still like cigarettes.

This situation could arise because the individual holds other evaluative beliefs which appear in other syllogisms (e.g., "Cigarettes relax me; I like being relaxed; therefore, I like cigarettes"). Even more likely, however, is the possibility that the attitude is only partially determined by its cognitive components. As noted above, emotional, behavioral, and social influences can also play important roles, and cognitive "reasoning" of the type represented in our syllogisms may be absent altogether. Certainly a man's devotion to cigarettes has few "cognitive" supports.

Thus, under our definition of an attitude as a like or a dislike, evaluative beliefs about an object may partially determine, but are not synonymous with, attitudes toward that object. Not only is it possible to like something which we evaluate negatively, such as cigarettes, but we may also dislike some things which we evaluate positively: I have only the highest regard for physical exercise, but . . .

VALUES

Just as an individual's higher-order beliefs can be traced back down through their syllogistic structures to their origins in first-order and zero-order primitive beliefs, so, too, higher-order attitudes are often found to rest upon basic values. For example, suppose that an individual who has a positive attitude toward money were asked to explain why. His justification might translate into a syllogistic structure of the form:

> Money would allow me to retire.
> I would like to retire.
> Therefore, I like money.

And when asked why he wants to retire:

> Retirement would allow me to take music lessons.
> I would like to take music lessons.
> Therefore, I would like to retire.

When pushed further:

> Music lessons would help me attain self-fulfillment.
> Self-fulfillment is desirable.
> Therefore, I would like to take music lessons.

Further questioning would reveal that the end of the syllogistic chain had been reached. That is, the evaluative belief "self-fulfillment is desirable" (or, alternatively, the attitude statement "I would like self-fulfillment") would be seen by the individual as an end in itself, and unlike money or retirement it would not be treated as a means to some other goal. No logical justification for wanting self-fulfillment would be seen as necessary or even possible; its desirability is self-evident. This is, of course, just a special case of what has been defined earlier in this book as a primitive belief; in this case, the primitive belief happens to be an attitude, or an evaluative belief. More concisely, then, a value is a primitive preference for or a positive attitude toward certain end-states of existence (like equality, salvation, self-fulfillment, or freedom) or certain broad modes of conduct (like courage, honesty, friendship, or chastity). (See Rokeach, 1968.) Values are ends, not means, and their desirability is either nonconsciously taken for granted (a zero-order belief) or seen as a direct derivation from one's experience or from some external authority (a first-order belief). To know whether a positive attitude or an evaluative belief is also a value for a particular individual, one must know the functional role it plays in his total belief system. One man's higher-order attitude can be another man's value. Money is a good example; it is a means to other values for most individuals, but an end in itself for some.

THE CENTRALITY OF VALUES: FREEDOM AND EQUALITY

Values are important because of their centrality to other beliefs and attitudes. That is, they enter as premises into many syllogisms, and accordingly, many particular attitudes and beliefs derive from them. This largely accounts for the fact that the same clusters of opinions appear so frequently in our society. Labels like "liberal" and "conservative" usually enable us to predict many of an individual's attitudes because these two terms refer to broad underlying values which are shared by large segments of the population. In fact, most of us, liberals and conservatives alike, share many of the same values, and our differences of opinion stem from the relative importance we assign to them. This is nicely illustrated in a series of studies by Milton Rokeach.

Rokeach (1968) asked a number of individuals to rank twelve values in the order of the values' importance to them. The values included such things as *wisdom, a comfortable life, a world at peace, salvation, maturity,* and so forth. Rokeach was particularly interested in differences among individuals who attached different degrees of importance to the values *freedom* and *equality.* For example, he obtained such rankings from individuals who had participated in civil rights demonstrations, from individuals who had not participated but who were sympathetic to them, and from individuals who were unsympathetic to them. Table 1 shows how each of these groups ranked the two values *freedom* and *equality* in the list of twelve.

Table 1

Rank of freedom *and* equality *in relation to civil rights attitudes. (Adapted from Rokeach, 1968, p. 170.)*

	PARTICIPATED	SYMPATHETIC	UNSYMPATHETIC
FREEDOM	1	1	2
EQUALITY	3	6	11

It is seen in Table 1 that *freedom* ranks high for all three groups, but *equality* is considered relatively unimportant (next to last among the twelve values) for those unsympathetic to civil rights demonstrations. This last pattern is almost identical to that obtained from fifty policemen in a midwestern city who ranked *freedom* first but *equality* last. Similarly, unemployed whites ranked *freedom* third and *equality* ninth. One begins to appreciate the depth of the racial split in our society when one compares these groups with a group of unemployed Negroes: they ranked *freedom* tenth and *equality* first!

If values like *freedom* and *equality* are really central to our belief systems, then they should underlie political views far broader than just racial ones. This is certainly Rokeach's view. For example, he suggests that we can think of many political orientations in terms of these two values as shown in Figure 1.

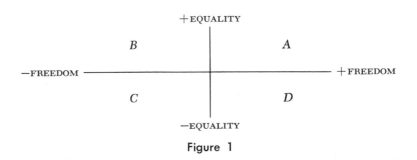

Figure 1

In this figure, individuals who value both *equality* and *freedom* positively as compared to other values will fall into the quadrant marked *A*. According to Rokeach, liberal Democrats, socialists, and humanists fit such a description. Stalinist and Maoist communists fall into quadrant *B;* they value *equality* much more than they value *freedom.* Quadrant *C* would seem to characterize fascists, Nazis, and members of the Ku Klux Klan, all of whom appear to place a low value on both *freedom* and *equality.* Finally, Rokeach places conservative Republicans, followers of Ayn Rand, and members of the John Birch Society in quadrant *D;* they value *freedom* more than they value *equality.*

Rokeach has some evidence to back up his classifications. He and a colleague, James Morrison, selected political writings representative of what they believed the four quadrants to be. They drew 25,000-word samples from socialist writers like Norman Thomas and Erich Fromm. Other samples were taken from such books as Lenin's *Collected Works,* Hitler's *Mein Kampf,* and Goldwater's *Conscience of a Conservative.* They then counted the number of times that seventeen different values, including *freedom* and *equality,* were mentioned in each sample. Finally, they ranked the seventeen values for each selection in terms of the number of favorable references minus the number of unfavorable references. For example, the socialists mentioned *freedom* favorably 66 times and *equality* favorably 62 times; for them, *freedom* ranked first and *equality* second in relative frequency of favorable mention among the 17 values. Table 2 shows the rankings for all four groups. Notice how nicely Rokeach's hypotheses are supported.

Table 2

Rank of freedom *and* equality *in writings by socialists, Lenin, Hitler, and Goldwater. (Adapted from Rokeach, 1968, p. 172.)*

	SOCIALISTS (A)	LENIN (B)	HITLER (C)	GOLDWATER (D)
FREEDOM	1	17	16	1
EQUALITY	2	1	17	16

NONCONSCIOUS VALUES: THE LOVE OF LIFE AND THE NEW POLITICS

Political scientists have noted that the one-dimensional liberal-conservative distinction is so oversimplified that it cannot account for the complexity of political ideologies. In this respect, then, Rokeach's differentiation of the political map into four quadrants on the basis of the familiar values of *freedom* and *equality* would seem to be an improvement. Certainly his categories make a good deal of intuitive sense, and they do seem to offer some additional insight into the differences between political ideologies.

But the primitive values that underlie a man's political views are not always the obvious or familiar ones, no matter how they are rearranged or combined. A number of psychologists believe that we must look more deeply into men's nonconscious and unconscious values if we hope to penetrate down to the actual set of primitive premises which generate their political views. This is exactly what a psychologist named Michael Maccoby did in order to understand the "new politics" which first emerged during the 1968 Presidential primary campaigns.

This new coalition of political sentiments first formed around the candidacy of Senator Eugene McCarthy when he decided to challenge the incumbent, President Johnson, for the Democratic presidential nomination on the issue of ending the war in Vietnam. McCarthy had little or no support from the traditional political machines and interest groups, but he attracted large groups of voters who cut across age groups, political parties, and all of the more traditional social, economic, and political lines. Although McCarthy appealed to many "liberals," it was clear that the "new politics" coalition could not be accurately characterized by any of the old familiar political labels. In particular, it was apparent that the liberal-versus-conservative distinction was no longer the most valid one. For this reason Maccoby decided to test a deeper, less obvious, distinction, a distinction based upon the thinking of the psychoanalyst Erich Fromm (1964), with whom Maccoby had previously collaborated.

Fromm's theory states that one of the basic dimensions of character is the "love of life versus the attraction to what is not alive (dead or mechanical)." According to Maccoby:

A person with intense love of life is attracted to that which is alive, which grows, which is free and unpredictable. He has an aversion to violence and all that destroys life. Thus he dislikes sterile and rigid order. He rejects being mechanized, becoming a lifeless part of machine-like organization. He enjoys life in all its manifestations in contrast to mere excitement or thrills. He believes in molding and influencing by love, reason and example rather than by force.

At the other pole, there are individuals attracted to that which is rigidly ordered, mechanical and unalive. These people do not like anything free and uncontrolled. They feel that people must be regulated within well-oiled machines. The extreme are those who are attracted to what is dead (1968, p. 2).

Of course, very few people are located at either extreme end of this dimension, and so Maccoby and Fromm constructed a 15-item questionnaire which would enable them to place individuals somewhere on the dimension between the two extremes. Some of the questions touched on whether the individual preferred rigid orderliness over sensual pleasures. (Is it more important for a wife to keep the house neat or to cook well?) Others probed whether the individual valued life over property. (If you saw a burglar running from your home with some of your valuables, would you shoot at him, call the police, or do nothing?) Still other questions were used to identify the small number of people on the extreme antilife end of the dimension (approximately 10%) who are actually attracted by death and matters related to it. (How many times a year should one visit the cemetery?) The questions were derived from psychoanalytic theory and clinical experience, and only those questions that survived various statistical testing procedures were included in the final questionnaire.

The full questionnaire was given to 160 persons living in California just prior to the presidential primary election there on June 4, 1968. The results showed that of those persons favoring McCarthy, 77% scored on the life-loving side of the median. No other candidate attracted a majority of such people. The percentages of those classified as life-loving who supported the other candidates were as follows: Nelson Rockefeller, 46%; Robert F. Kennedy, 34%; Richard Nixon, 27%; Hubert Humphrey, 24%; Ronald Reagan and George C. Wallace, 20%. In general, McCarthy supporters were drawn from "life-loving" individuals in all segments of the population, whereas support for the other candidates tended to break down along the more traditional social, economic, and political lines. Thus, for example, the late Robert Kennedy also appealed to many "life-lovers," but, more than McCarthy he also drew support based on these more traditional factors. Therefore the percentage of "life-lovers" among Kennedy supporters was lower.

Other results revealed that "life-loving" individuals emphasized ending poverty, stopping the war in Vietnam, aiding underdeveloped countries, and securing a guaranteed income for every American. "Anti-life" voters supported a tighter control of rioters, tighter enforcement of anti-drug laws, winning in Vietnam, controlling subversive groups, strengthening the police, and fighting communism.

Although I think this is a good study and have no reason to doubt the validity of its findings, Maccoby's descriptions of the two kinds of people is hardly a neutral one. It is clear that he (and Dr. Fromm) think that there are good guys and bad guys here. As it happens, my biases coincide with Maccoby's, but imagine his dismay if the same study had been reported by someone who, with a different political orientation, chose to call Maccoby's "life-lovers" the "bleeding-heart anarchists" and his "anti-lifers" the "pragmatic realists." Maccoby, more than incidentally, was an active campaigner in the California primary. Maccoby's presidential choice? That is left as an exercise for the reader.

UNCONSCIOUS VALUES: THE PREJUDICED PERSONALITY

Maccoby's study of the "new politics" is not the first case in which psychologists have turned to psychoanalytic thinking in order to better understand beliefs and attitudes. In fact, psychologists are likely to look to the psychoanalytic insights of Sigmund Freud first whenever an individual appears to hold certain beliefs and attitudes primarily to fulfill his own unconscious values, to satisfy his own unconscious needs, or to protect himself against unconscious threats to his own self-esteem.

It is not surprising, then, that the most ambitious attempt to apply psychoanalytic thinking to the area of beliefs and attitudes concerns the study of racial and religious prejudice. Psychoanalytic theory suggests that some prejudice may be a reflection of the individual's own insecurities; the highly prejudiced individual may be one who denies or represses his own weaknesses or aggressive and sexual needs and, in Freudian terms, "projects" them onto minority groups. That is, he then perceives such groups as weak, and yet threatening, aggressive, and sexually immoral; and he uses them as scapegoats, blaming any frustrating circumstances of his life upon them.

This theory was tested in the late 1940s by a group of psychologists at the University of California at Berkeley, two of whom had escaped to America from Nazi Germany. Specifically, they sought to discover whether this theory of prejudice could help to explain anti-Semitism. Their research, described fully in their book, *The Authori-*

tarian Personality (Adorno, Frenkel-Brunswick, Levinson & Sanford, 1950), revealed first that an individual who was highly anti-Semitic was also very likely to be prejudiced against many other minorities or "out-groups." This finding supported the investigators' hypothesis that the prejudice against Jews was a general prejudice in such individuals and could not simply be attributed to actual unpleasant encounters with Jews. Through the use of pencil-and-paper questionnaires, extensive interviews, and other psychological tests, the Berkeley investigators gradually evolved a personality portrait of the individual who was likely to be highly *ethnocentric*—that is, generally prejudiced against all out-groups.

In the interviews, the ethnocentric individual recalled harsh, threatening parental discipline, parental love which was contingent upon "good" behavior, a hierarchical family structure, and an anxious concern about family status. The nonethnocentric individual, on the other hand, reported reasonable parental discipline, unconditional parental love, an equalitarian family structure, and little or no concern over status.

From the first of these home environments, according to the Berkeley investigators, emerges the individual whom they call the "authoritarian personality." He sees the world divided into the weak and the strong and is power-oriented in his personal relationships—submissive and obedient to those he considers his superiors but contemptuous and authoritarian toward those he considers inferior. The nonauthoritarian, on the other hand, tends to be affectionate and love-oriented in his personal relationships. The authoritarian finds it difficult to tolerate ambiguity and tends to hold highly conventional values; there was some evidence that he is likely to be politically conservative. Although he tends to describe his parents in overly idealistic terms, he reveals deep unconscious resentments against them. The nonauthoritarian tends to hold a more balanced view of his parents, seeing both strengths and weaknesses.

As the psychoanalytic theory suggested, the authoritarian individual is fearful of the subjective and tends to reject psychological introspection of himself and psychological understanding of others as "prying into private matters." He cannot accept the possibility that he might be personally weak, aggressive, sexually motivated, or that he might possess any such undesirable qualities. Instead he "projects" such undesirable traits onto members of out-groups. We thus arrive at his racially prejudiced attitudes. The authoritarian individual, according to the Berkeley investigators, is the kind of person who would be particularly susceptible to the kind of fascist ideology that was seen in Nazi Germany.

The Berkeley investigation has become a classic in social psychological research, and even by today's standards, the project was an ambitious one. Furthermore, it has spawned an enormous amount of research utilizing the F scale, the pencil-and-paper questionnaire developed during the project to measure an individual's authoritarianism.

The Berkeley investigation has also been criticized; in fact, an entire book of criticism was published a few years after *The Authoritarian Personality* appeared (Christie & Jahoda, 1954). Many of the methods employed in the study were criticized, and it was pointed out that the investigators had not checked the possibility that lack of education, rather than the personality characteristics, accounted for some of the beliefs and attitudes of authoritarian individuals. Other critics felt that the investigators had captured only the authoritarians of the "right wing" and had missed authoritarians who might subscribe to left-wing ideology. Communists, for example, emerge as nonauthoritarians when measured by the F scale, but other research has indicated that many of them may share some of the rigidities of the authoritarian (Rokeach, 1960).

These and other criticisms of the study must be taken seriously, and we have learned to avoid many of the mistakes made by the pioneering Berkeley group. But still, many of the original results have withstood the test of continued research, and many psychologists, myself included, believe that the general conclusions of the study are still tenable. It would appear that at least some racial and religious prejudice can be partially explained by the psychoanalytic theory proposed by the Berkeley group. There do appear to be individuals with "authoritarian personalities," individuals who seem particularly susceptible to a fascist ideology which has hostility toward minority groups at its core.

The area of beliefs and attitudes is not the only area of social psychology which has been illuminated by Freudian thought. It is true that not all of psychoanalytic theory has been adequately validated, that parts of it clearly need further correction or modification, and that, in its present form at least, it cannot explain all of human behavior satisfactorily. Nevertheless, it remains to this day our most comprehensive single theory of human thought and behavior. In a very real sense, we are all Freudians; Freudian concepts and insights have become so much a part of our thinking that their influence is now largely nonconscious. Even parents who have done nothing more than raise their children with the occasional guidance of Dr. Spock are more like Freudian psychologists than they might care to know.[1]

[1] A more complete exposition of the psychoanalytic viewpoint will be found in Blum, *Psychodynamics: The Science of Unconscious Mental Forces*, 1966, in this series. A more technical discussion of psychoanalytic theory as it applies to attitudes appears in Sarnoff (1960).

In Chapter 2, I mentioned briefly that underlying the syllogistic description of beliefs and attitudes is the notion that individuals possess coherent systems of beliefs and attitudes which are internally consistent, and that this idea has also been central to a number of recent psychological theories. These "cognitive consistency" theories have generated most of the research on beliefs and attitudes in the past decade and have supplied much of the evidence upon which my presentation is implicitly based.

Most of the cognitive consistency theorists have been interested primarily in the process of belief and attitude *change*. They reason that men possess a drive toward cognitive consistency, and that, therefore, inconsistency acts as an irritant or stimulus which motivates individuals to change their beliefs and attitudes, to bring any maverick premises or conclusions "into line." It follows from this reasoning that one should be able to change an individual's beliefs or attitudes by exposing or creating inconsistencies among them. This is, in fact, the procedure that most of the cognitive consistency theorists have employed in order to test their theories.

An example of consistency theory research which is closely related to the syllogistic description of beliefs and attitudes was conducted by a psychologist named William McGuire (1960). McGuire prepared a questionnaire containing 48 propositions which had been taken from 16 syllogisms. For example, three of the propositions were drawn from the syllogism:

> Any form of recreation that constitutes a serious health menace will be outlawed by the City Health Authority.
> The increasing water pollution in this area will make swimming a serious health menace.
> Swimming at the local beaches will be outlawed by the City Health Authority.

On the questionnaire, the propositions did not appear in syllogistic form. Instead, they were dispersed within the questionnaire among propositions from other syllogisms and filler items.

High school students were asked to fill out the questionnaire by indicating their belief in the truth of each proposition on a numerical scale. About a week later, these students received persuasive messages arguing for the truth of each of the 16 minor premises (the first premise of each syllogism); the messages did not mention either the major premises (the second premise of each syllogism) or the conclusions. After receiving the messages, the students again indicated their beliefs about the 48 propositions. Finally, they indicated their beliefs for the third time a week later.

The results showed that immediately after the persuasion there was not only a significant change toward a greater belief in the propositions explicitly mentioned in the persuasive messages, as might be expected, but also a significant, though smaller, change toward a greater belief in the unmentioned conclusions. This is, of course, what the cognitive consistency theory would predict: if one changes a premise somewhere in the vertical structure of a belief, the drive for consistency will motivate a change in any higher-order beliefs that rest upon that premise. One week later, McGuire found that the effects of the persuasion on the propositions discussed in the messages had diminished, but that most of the stronger belief in the conclusions had been retained. McGuire suggests that this shows a kind of mental inertia; the change originally induced on the minor premises continued to "filter down" to the conclusions during the intervening week and partly overcame the fading of the effects of the persuasion.

In a related study, McGuire found that persuasion itself is not always necessary. He reports that merely having the subjects fill out the questionnaire caused them to adjust their beliefs so that one week later there was somewhat greater consistency between their belief in the premises and their belief in the conclusions. Similarly, he found that persuasive messages were more effective if they attempted to push the individual's beliefs toward greater consistency than toward inconsistency. All of these findings provide support for the general cognitive consistency hypothesis. It should be mentioned, however, that this hypothesis may not always hold, and some subsequent studies have failed to find the persuasion filtering down through the syllogism as the theory requires.

McGuire's studies examined the consistency within single syllogisms containing nonevaluative beliefs. Other consistency theorists have looked for *attitude* consistency as well, and some have investigated consistency across syllogisms as well as consistency within single syllogisms. For example, a number of researchers have used numerical scales and algebraic formulae to demonstrate that an individual's higher-order attitudes can be predicted by combining the horizontal and vertical syllogisms which contain the relevant underlying beliefs and values (e.g., Fishbein, 1963; Peak, 1955; Rosenberg, 1956, 1960; Zajonc, 1954).

The hypothesis that change in belief can be produced by exposing or creating inconsistencies within the belief system has also been validated in several experiments dealing specifically with values and attitudes. For example, Rokeach (1968) attempted to arouse feelings of attitude and value inconsistency in college students to see if attitude or value change would occur.

First Rokeach obtained the students' value ratings and their views on equal rights and civil rights demonstrations. Then he showed them that, on the average, they had ranked *freedom* first and *equality* sixth. He also showed them the low ranking given to *equality* by those who were unsympathetic to civil rights demonstrations. The subjects were then told: "This suggests that Michigan State students in general are more interested in their own freedom than they are in freedom for other people . . . [and] this raises the question as to whether those who are against civil rights are really saying that they care a great deal about their own freedom but are indifferent to other people's freedom. Those who are for civil rights are perhaps really saying that they not only want freedom for themselves but for other people too." The subjects were invited to think about their own value rankings and attitudes in this light. They were asked to rank their values and state their attitudes again three weeks later and once again three to five months later.

The results of this experiment are generally what the consistency hypothesis would predict. Little attitude change was found among students who were already consistent; that is, students who ranked *equality* high and were pro–civil rights and students who ranked *equality* low and were anti–civil rights did not change their attitudes. (The latter group did raise its ranking of *equality* somewhat, however.) On the other hand, those who ranked *equality* high but who were initially anti–civil rights increased their liberalism on the civil rights issues dramatically, while retaining the importance of *equality* in their value rankings. Thus, exposing the inconsistency between their value rankings and their attitudes motivated attitude change, as the consistency hypothesis predicted. Interestingly, a delay effect similar to the one reported by McGuire in his syllogism study was also found: the change in civil rights attitudes was greater after three to five months than it was only three weeks after the experiment. Again, the changes apparently needed time to filter down through the syllogistic structure. Finally, students who had initially ranked *equality* low but were pro–civil rights dramatically raised the importance of *equality* in their value rankings and retained their pro–civil rights attitudes.

Perhaps you have noticed that Rokeach's subjects could also have resolved their inconsistencies by lowering the importance of *equality* in their rankings or, for this last group, by becoming more opposed to civil rights. That is, the attitude and value changes that Rokeach observed in his study were in the "socially desirable" direction, a result that the consistency hypothesis itself does not predict. This would seem to indicate that social pressure was operating rather strongly in these experiments, which leaves open the possibility that social pressure rather than inconsistency was responsible for *all* the changes. To be certain that this was not the case, we would have to show that we could change attitudes and values in the socially undesirable direction with this technique, a procedure that many psychologists, including Rokeach, might hesitate to try for ethical reasons.

CONSISTENCY AND RATIONALITY

To say that a man is consistent is not necessarily to say that he is logical or rational, and almost every example I have cited confirms the reality of this distinction between psycho-logic and logic. In fact, only McGuire's study of belief syllogisms seems to demonstrate a strictly logical kind of consistency. But when McGuire looked at his subjects' attitudes as well as their beliefs, he too found some interesting psychological consistencies that logic could not explain.

Thus, when McGuire asked his subjects to rate the desirability of each of the 48 propositions employed in his study, he found that there was a high correlation between these ratings and the degree to which the subjects believed the propositions to be true. That is, the more his subjects believed something to be true, on the average, the more they thought it to be desirable. Furthermore, when the degree of belief in a proposition changed as a result of McGuire's persuasion, the desirability of the proposition also changed. This, then, is a kind of consistency we might call "rationalization." If we come to believe that something is true, then we persuade ourselves that it is desirable as well. McGuire suggests that the reverse sequence of reasoning could also take place: because we believe something to be desirable, we persuade ourselves that it is true. We usually call this "wishful thinking." Both rationalization and wishful thinking could account for the correlation between belief ratings and desirability ratings observed prior to the persuasion. Both produce a consistency, not of logic, but of psycho-logic.

Rationalization and wishful thinking were also shown by the consistency theorist Milton Rosenberg (1960). Rosenberg began with the perverse idea that he might be able to work backwards, so to speak, to change the underlying beliefs and values in a syllogism by altering the higher-order attitude first. For example, one might be able to alter the premises in the following syllogism by first changing the conclusion:

Negroes moving into white neighborhoods will lower
property values.
It is desirable to have property values well protected.
Therefore, it is undesirable to have Negroes move into
white neighborhoods.

To perform this exotic feat, Rosenberg first measured the beliefs,
values, and attitudes of his subjects; then he hypnotized them and told
them that they would have certain attitudes when they awoke. For
example, a subject might be told: "When you awake you will be very
much in favor of Negroes moving into white neighborhoods. The mere
idea . . . will give you a happy, exhilarated feeling. Although you will
not remember this suggestion having been made, it will strongly influence your feelings after you have awakened" (pp. 26–27). Notice
that nothing was said about any of the belief or value premises that
might underlie attitudes toward integrated neighborhoods.

The results confirmed Rosenberg's hunch. Under the effect of the
posthypnotic suggestion, subjects showed changes in their underlying
belief premises. For example, after the experiment, they would be
inclined to see integrated neighborhoods as less likely to lower property
values. Some subjects also altered the importance of the underlying
value premises. Thus an individual who had earlier rated maintenance
of property values as very important now saw it as less important.
Finally, Rosenberg reports that some of the "cognitive reorganization"
that took place under the influence of the posthypnotic suggestion remained even after the suggestion was removed. Thus, Rosenberg's study
demonstrates, too, a resolution of inconsistency that is not strictly
logical. When an individual alters his perception of reality to corre-
spond with what he sees as desirable, we usually do not say that he is
rational, but that he is rationalizing or thinking wishfully.

ALTERNATIVE PATHS TO CONSISTENCY

Inconsistency is not always resolved by bringing the maverick beliefs, attitudes, or values into line. At least four other strategies for
reducing inconsistency have been distinguished: denial, bolstering, differentiation, and transcendence (Abelson, 1959). To illustrate, we can
consider the recent plight of the liberal-intellectual who believes in
racial integration but also finds himself in sympathy with the Black
Power movement, a movement which includes many separatist aspects.

First, he can *deny* one of the troublesome beliefs involved: "Black
power is really just another name for the older integrationist, civil
rights goals." Second, he can *bolster* one of the attitudes by seeking out
other supportive beliefs and thus attempt to swamp the inconsistency:
"Black power will accomplish many other important goals even if it is

incompatible with racial integration." A third strategy is to *differentiate* one of the belief objects into separate parts: "Black power really contains two separable aspects, one dealing with enhanced human pride; the other, with separatism. One can subscribe to one without endorsing the other." Finally, he can employ the strategy of *transcendence*, a kind of reverse differentiation in that it sees the two disparate beliefs as part of a larger, or transcendent, unity: "Black power is a temporary tactic for fulfilling the ultimate goal of integration, and both derive from the more basic values of self-determination and shared power for all men." Other inconsistency-reducing strategies have also been suggested by other psychologists. (See McGuire, 1966, for a brief review of these.) As this example illustrates again, the path to consistency may or may not respect the canons of logic and evidence.

HIDDEN CONSISTENCY

As we have seen in the case of the "new politics," the primitive beliefs and values that underlie a man's higher-order attitudes may not always be the familiar or obvious ones. Thus, in real life, it might be a gross error to charge someone with "valuing his own freedom but not the freedom of others" just because he ranks *freedom* first among his values but opposes civil rights activities. His attitudes toward civil rights may well rest upon a syllogistic structure based upon very different premises altogether. More generally, before we accuse a man of being inconsistent we should make sure that the alleged inconsistencies are not just in the eyes of us beholders, beholders who are simply ignorant of the actual premises underlying the belief system. Two cases will serve to illustrate my point: the racial attitudes of some American Christians and the political orientation of most behavioral scientists.

FREE WILL AND THE RACIAL ATTITUDES OF CHRISTIANS

The central doctrines and beliefs of Christianity would appear to provide basic premises upon which Christians could base racial tolerance, compassion, and understanding. Certainly this is the predominant view of the Christian churches. Thus, all the major religious denominations in America, Christian and otherwise, have taken outspoken stands against racial prejudice, citing their religious beliefs as the basis for their positions. Racial prejudice, each of these churches has asserted, is a cluster of attitudes which is ethically incompatible and logically inconsistent with the central religious teachings of the faith.

An examination of the predominant attitudes of the Christian clergy in America supports this claim. Studies have shown that only about one out of ten Protestant ministers and Roman Catholic diocesan priests opposes or disapproves of the civil rights movement (Hadden, 1969;

Fichter, 1968). More than 75% of the Protestant clergy in the Hadden study thought that the churches had been inadequate in facing up to civil rights issues, and a large majority favored direct action by the churches on these issues. Nor are the clergy the only individuals who base racial tolerance on the moral teachings of the New Testament. Two sociologists, Rodney Stark and Charles Glock (1968), have found that individuals who hold a firm commitment to the ethics of Christianity are much less likely to hold religious and racial prejudices than individuals who lack such a commitment.

But here's the catch: Stark and Glock also found that the commitment to Christian ethics is unrelated to other forms of Christian commitment. Church members who accepted the other historically orthodox doctrines of the church or who regularly attended church or participated in church activities were *less* likely to accept Christian ethics than those who were less orthodox in their beliefs and less regular in their participation. In other words, when the churches look for support for their ethical teachings, they are more likely to find it among their most inactive members than among those who fill the pews. A California study (Glock & Stark, 1966) showed that although 91% of both Catholic and Protestant church members agreed that "love thy neighbor means that we should treat all races the same" and felt that "Negroes ought to have the same rights and opportunities as others," nearly a third said on the same page of the questionnaire that they did not want Negroes in their churches. Over 40% would move if Negro families moved into their block; a third thought Negroes were less intelligent than whites; and nearly a half blamed communists and other radicals for racial tension. A national survey (Hadden, 1969) showed that 89% of the Christian laity felt that Negroes ought to take advantage of the opportunities society offers them and quit their protesting. And again, this percentage was substantially lower only among those Christians who rarely or never attended church.

The views of the Christian laity are thus sharply divergent from the views of their clergy and from the official positions of their churches. Moreover, the contemporary Christian churchgoer strongly opposes the role being played by the churches to overcome prejudice. Thus, 70% of the laity in the national study denounced clerical involvement in social issues such as civil rights, and many other studies indicate that the majority of laymen want their church to stick to tending the private religious needs of its members and to stay out of such questions as peace, justice, and human rights. It is true, of course, that social action is a major activity of a few denominations and that individual instances of racial tolerance can be found in most churches, but the fact remains that these active denominations and these committed individuals are not in the majority.

It is clear, then, that the Christian ethical base which could serve as the central set of premises for racial tolerance does not appear to fulfill that role for the bulk of Christian churchgoers in America. But this does *not* imply that the Christian churchgoers are necessarily being inconsistent. Instead, Stark and Glock (1968) suggest that there are other central beliefs in Christian doctrine which—when interpreted by the layman at least—contribute to racial prejudice rather than diminish it. The most central of these beliefs appears to be a radical version of the freewill conception of man.

The freewill conception of man sees him as a free actor, essentially capable of rising above the circumstances of his environment by virtue of his own efforts, free to choose and thus free to effect his own salvation. In general terms, this conception of man underlies traditional Christian thought and is central to the doctrines of sin and salvation. For only if a man is considered to be in control of and responsible for his own destiny do the notions of punishment for sin and the need for repentance make theological—as opposed to psychological—sense. Western societies are built largely upon this general conception of man.

In the modern world, the radical version of unfettered man has been modified, and most theologians and clergymen hold relatively sophisticated versions of this general conception. But a great many Christian laymen adhere to it in its most pristine form, and these laymen are concentrated among the most active church members (Stark & Glock, 1969). Their radical freewill belief leads them to a conservative view of civil rights issues (and many other issues) because it leads them to put the blame for disadvantage upon those who are disadvantaged. Accordingly, these laymen tend to be oblivious to the external forces which may dominate the circumstances of the disadvantaged and tend to see political and social efforts on behalf of the disadvantaged as irrelevant at best. As Stark and Glock point out, it is not that these Christians condone the social forces that deprive black Americans or other minority groups, but that they do not recognize the existence or extent of such forces. They recognize that black Americans, for example, are collectively disadvantaged, but the conclusion that follows from their radical freewill belief is that such a collective shortcoming must be a racial trait. And to the extent that Christian institutions support such a radical view of individual freedom and accountability, their members can be expected to reject the very premises upon which the argument against prejudice and discrimination rests. The disadvantaged condition of minority groups proves their unworthiness, and there is no reason to support measures to help them.

One fact we should not overlook is that many black Americans are also Christians. Just as some white Americans see Christian ethics as the basis of their commitment to racial justice and equality, so too, many black Christians see their religious beliefs as the logical basis of the kind of civil rights activism epitomized by the late Dr. Martin Luther King, Jr. But even in the black community, the central belief in the freewill conception of man plays a countervailing role. In a study of militancy in the black community, a strong negative correlation was found between religious commitment and the desire for justice and equality (Marx, 1967). That is, the more a black respondent was committed to Christian beliefs and institutions, the more likely he was to view the deprived conditions of most black Americans as having been caused by their own fault. Two thirds of the urban blacks in the sample studied believed that "Negroes who want to work hard can get ahead just as easily as anyone else," and about half of the sample thought that "Before Negroes are given equal rights, they have to show that they deserve them."

The freewill conception of man is not the only theological premise which Stark and Glock uncovered in their studies. Often allied with this premise was the belief that social reform takes place only through divine intervention, and this too reinforces opposition to efforts to improve the conditions of the disadvantaged. And again, this belief is a basic premise for some black Americans. About one third of the Northern urban blacks and more than one half of the Southern urban blacks in the study mentioned above (Marx, 1967) thought that "Negroes should spend more time praying and less time demonstrating." One Negro clergyman summed it up by saying, "Praying is demonstrating."

Thus, rather than concluding that the majority of Christian churchgoers are inconsistent, we should recognize that, in their eyes, if there is any contradiction here, it is a contradiction between the church's doctrines and its own efforts to effect social change!

DETERMINISM AND THE POLITICAL ORIENTATION OF BEHAVIORAL SCIENTISTS

Behavioral scientists provide a second example of an identifiable group of people whose conception of man generates a system of higher-order beliefs and attitudes. Furthermore, their working conception of man is the direct opposite of the freewill conception discussed above. Thus, just as the physical scientist assumes that the phenomena he studies are governed by principles of cause and effect, and hence are not under the influence of capricious forces or "freewill," so too, most behavioral scientists take a more-or-less deterministic view of human behavior. It is their working assumption that the causes of human thought and action are to be found ultimately in the genetic background or the social environment of the individual, not in his soul or his free will. The existence of the individual's own "willpower" is not denied, but it too is assumed to be a product or creation of his earlier training and of other external influences beyond his own control. To a behavioral scientist, for example, the explanation that a particular black man will not work because he lacks willpower or because he is lazy is no explanation at all; the working assumption of determinism obligates the scientist to ask the further question: "What are the environmental conditions that deprive a man of his motivation to work?"

Since this conception of man sensitizes behavioral scientists to the kinds of environmental variables that are under the potential control of man for improving his own lot, it is not surprising that they are among the strongest advocates of action programs for social change. The familiar charge of those on the extreme political right that all behavioral scientists are communists and atheists is, shall we say, exaggerated, but it is true that psychologists, sociologists, and political scientists are politically to the left of most Americans, and they are not conspicuously religious either.

Thus, whereas approximately 44% of the national adult population in America consider themselves Democrats (Gallup poll, December, 1966), a national survey of behavioral scientists at academic institutions showed that identification with the Democratic party ran from a low of 70% among psychologists, through 74% for political scientists, to a high of 78% among sociologists (McClintock, Spaulding, & Turner, 1965). (Since identification with the Republican party among these groups was 21%, 16%, and 10% respectively, that really doesn't leave many recruits for the Communist party—unless, of course, some of them are using the two major parties as fronts!) Of course, identification with the Democratic party has never been a surefire index of political liberalism, but a separate measure of political ideology in this same survey confirmed that behavioral scientists are clearly to the left of most Americans politically, with the sociologists being the most liberal, political scientists next, and psychologists last among the three professions. And although the figures are not given separately, I would guess that social psychologists, the psychologists most likely to be consulted on social issues, would resemble the sociologists more than they would resemble other psychologists.

With regard to religious belief, about half the sociologists and about two thirds of the psychologists indicated either that they were not religious or that they did not consider religion a major force in their lives. Political scientists were slightly more likely to consider themselves at least "moderately" religious. But just as there do not appear to be many Communists, neither are there very many atheists. Only 15% of the psychologists, the least religious of the three groups, indicated "none" when asked for religious preference. Public decision-makers take note. This is what we're like.

THE CASE FOR NONCONSISTENCY

Up to this point, I have tried to state the strongest possible case for the thesis that men do not merely subscribe to a random collection of beliefs and attitudes but rather possess coherent *systems* of beliefs and attitudes which are internally and psychologically consistent. I have even implied that whenever an individual's beliefs and attitudes appear to be inconsistent, if we would only look deeper into the basic premises of his belief system, consistency will be forthcoming.

We have seen that the consistency theorists themselves have taken the further step of postulating that men possess a drive toward cognitive consistency. As I have done, these theorists emphasize that this consistency is most often psychological rather than logical, and they are alert to the nonrationality of some of the strategies which individuals often employ to attain consistency. In addition, consistency theorists do not claim that individuals need to be aware of the inconsistencies in order to be motivated toward consistency. The consistency theorists are thus quite flexible, and collectively they have marshaled an impressive amount of evidence to document their main hypothesis that inconsistency motivates belief and attitude change. Indeed, a recently published book called *Theories of Cognitive Consistency: A Sourcebook* (known affectionately by the in-group as TOCCAS) contains 84 chapters, 830 pages of text, 41 pages of references (about 1000 references), and more about cognitive consistency than almost anyone would care to know (Abelson, Aronson, McGuire, Newcomb, Rosenberg, & Tannenbaum, 1968). Inconsistency, they seem to be trying to tell us, motivates belief and attitude change.

But I don't believe it. At least not very much. In my view, a vision of inconsistency as a temporary turbulence in an otherwise fastidious pool of cognitive clarity is all too misleading. My own suspicion is that inconsistency is probably our most enduring cognitive commonplace. That is, I suspect that for most of the people most of the time and for all the people some of the time inconsistency just sits there. I think that we academic psychologists, including the consistency theorists, probably spend too much time with bright college students who are as eager to achieve a respectable overall unity in their cognitions as we, their instructors, are eager to impress them and ourselves with the same admirable coherence of thought. We have already seen that we psychologists are well represented in the population of liberal-intellectuals who are willing to spend restless nights agonizing over the apparent inconsistencies between integration and black power, and you will find us striving for cognitive quiescence on similar dilemmas at any meeting of the American Civil Liberties Union. I believe, in short, that there is more inconsistency on earth (and probably in heaven) than is dreamt of in our psychological theories.

Psychologists and political scientists who have analyzed the public mind outside the laboratory have arrived at similar conclusions. For example, Herbert McClosky, a man who has spent much time trying to understand the political attitudes of Americans, has said, "As intellectuals and students of politics we are disposed by training and sensibility to take political ideas seriously. . . . We are therefore prone to forget that most people take them less seriously than we do, that they pay little attention to issues, rarely worry about the consistency of their opinions, and spend little or no time thinking about the values, presuppositions and implications which distinguish one political orientation from another." (Quoted by Abelson, 1968.) Let me illustrate.

LIBERALS OR CONSERVATIVES?

Lloyd Free, a pollster and political analyst, and Hadley Cantril, a social psychologist, have conducted a large-scale study of the political beliefs of Americans (1967). Using the resources of the Gallup polling organization, these two men in 1964 interviewed over 3,000 people representing a cross-section of the American public. One of their purposes was to study the nature of liberalism and conservatism, both at a practical, or operational, level and at a more ideological level. First they constructed a five-item questionnaire to identify what they called operational liberalism and conservatism. It covered most of the controversial "welfare" programs of the Democratic administration then in office, including federal aid to education, Medicare, federal low-rent housing programs, urban renewal programs, and federal attempts to reduce unemployment. An individual was then defined as completely or predominantly liberal if he favored all or all but one of the programs on which he had an opinion. To qualify as completely or predominantly conservative, an individual had to oppose all or all but one of the programs on which he had an opinion. Others, providing that they had an opinion on at least three of the programs, were labeled as "middle-of-the-road."

The American public distributed itself as follows:

Completely or predominantly liberal	65%
Middle-of-the-road	21%
Completely or predominantly conservative	14%

In other words, about two thirds of the American public qualified as "liberal" with respect to the favoring of specific government programs; and within the liberal category itself, over two thirds of the individuals were "completely liberal" in that they favored all the government programs about which they had an opinion. As the table shows, only 14% of the American public could be labeled conservative at the operational level.

These results are in line with previous polls which show that the American public has been "liberal" in this sense at least since the days of the New Deal three decades ago. Even though "conservative" shifts of other kinds have occasionally intervened (e.g., with respect to civil rights activity) and though the 1966 and 1968 elections were interpreted by some as a trend toward conservatism, the general liberal trend toward welfare programs has never changed. Thus, a poll in February, 1967, showed that 54% of the American public favored even the controversial Community Action programs to combat poverty. The Head Start schooling program for young children was favored by 67%, and federally financed job training was endorsed by 75% of the American public; majorities also opposed any reduction in current programs involving federal grants for low-income housing and for welfare and relief payments. When it comes right down to the specifics of the welfare state, Americans are, for the most part, "liberals."

But what about ideology? What about the conservatives who supported Barry Goldwater in 1964 or voted for the conservative candidates in 1966 and 1968? Surely more than 14% of the American people are "conservative." And surely they are, as Free and Cantril discovered on a second questionnaire designed to identify not operational, but ideological, liberals and conservatives by asking the following questions:

1. The federal government is interfering too much in state and local matters.

2. The government has gone too far in regulating business and interfering with the free enterprise system.

3. Social problems here in this country could be solved more effectively if the government would only keep its hands off and let people in local communities handle their own problems in their own ways.

4. Generally speaking, any able-bodied person who really wants to work in this country can find a job and earn a living.

5. We should rely more on individual initiative and ability and not so much on governmental welfare programs.

A person had to disagree with all or all but one of the statements on which he had an opinion to qualify as completely or predominantly liberal on this "ideological" scale. To be defined as completely or predominantly conservative, he had to agree with all or all but one of the items on which he had an opinion. Others were classified as middle-of-the-road if they had an opinion on at least three statements. Table 3 shows the results of the ideological part of the survey in comparison with the operational part.

Table 3

Comparison of results on ideological and operational scales. (Adapted from Free & Cantril, 1967, p. 32.)

	IDEOLOGICAL SCALE	OPERATIONAL SCALE
Completely or predominantly liberal	16%	65%
Middle-of-the-road	34%	21%
Completely or predominantly conservative	50%	14%

As we see, a very different picture emerges. Half the American public is conservative in ideology, whereas only 14% of the American public would have the government pull out of any of its major welfare activities. Conversely, whereas 65% of Americans are liberal at the operational level, only 16% were either completely or predominantly liberal ideologically. Somebody here has cognitive schizophrenia.

We can identify that "somebody" by combining the results of the survey into a single table which shows how each group on the ideological scale stood on the operational scale.

Table 4

Operational scale and ideological scale combined. (Adapted from Free & Cantril, 1967, p. 37.)

	IDEOLOGICAL SCALE		
	Liberal	Middle-of-the-road	Conservative
OPERATIONAL SCALE			
Liberal	90%	78%	46%
Middle-of-the-road	9%	18%	28%
Conservative	1%	4%	26%

Table 4 shows that 90% of the ideological liberals also qualified as liberals on the operational scale, but among ideological conservatives almost half (46%) proved to be operational liberals! Another way of stating this result is to say that nearly one out of every four Americans (23%, that is, 46% of 50%) is an ideological conservative and at the same time an operational liberal. Barry Goldwater might have fared much better in 1964 if he could have attacked government programs in general while avoiding mention of any program in particular. The Republicans had apparently learned this lesson well by 1968, when Richard Nixon continued to make many ideologically conservative statements, just like those on the questionnaire, while at the same time proposing such things as increased Social Security benefits.

There is one flaw in the Free-Cantril study. Perhaps you noticed that the way all the questions were worded, anyone who agreed or approved of statements on the operational scale would be classified as "liberal" whereas anyone who agreed with statements on the ideological scale would be classified as "conservative." Consequently, a person who tends to agree with any plausible-sounding statement without examining it critically would automatically end up being inconsistent in this study. Indeed, research shows that such individuals do exist; they are called "yea-sayers" (Couch & Kenniston, 1960). I think it is quite likely that many of the individuals in the Free-Cantril study who ended up being classified as both ideological conservatives and operational liberals were simply pleasant people who tended to agree with anything the nice man said that seemed reasonable; they were yea-sayers. Perhaps it is more accurate to say that such people are nonconsistent or nonlogical rather than that they are inconsistent or illogical.

Of course, for purposes of my argument it doesn't matter why so many Americans ended up simultaneously as ideological conservatives and operational liberals. Whether they are truly inconsistent or simply nonconsistent (yea-sayers), the fact remains that at least 23% of the American people, unlike the intellectuals who make up consistency theories, "pay little attention to issues, rarely worry about the consistency of their opinions, and spend little or no time thinking about the values, presuppositions and implications which distinguish one political orientation from another."

Thus, I would suggest that consistency theories are all right in their place, but what we need is a good theory of nonconsistency. And when such needs arise, I consult Robert Abelson, the psychologist with theories for all occasions.[1]

OPINION MOLECULES: TOWARD A THEORY OF NONCONSISTENCY

Abelson (1968) suggests that an individual's beliefs and attitudes are often composed of encapsulated, isolated "opinion molecules." Each molecule is made up of (1) a belief, (2) an attitude, and (3) a perception of social support for them. Or, as Abelson likes to put it, each opinion molecule contains a fact, a feeling, and a following. For example: "It's a fact that when my Uncle Charlie had back trouble, he was cured by a chiropractor [fact]. You know, I feel that chiropractors have been sneered at too much [feeling], and I'm not ashamed to say so because

---

[1]Abelson has already been cited in this book as one of the men who coined the word psycho-logic, as the discoverer of alternative strategies for removing inconsistency, and as an editor of the cognitive consistency sourcebook. He is often considered to be a consistency theorist. Fortunately, he would rather be right than consistent.

I know a lot of people who feel the same way [*following*]." Or, "Nobody on this block wants to sell to Negroes [*following*], and neither do I [*feeling*]. The property values would decline [*fact*]."

Opinion molecules serve such a simple function that psychologists have usually ignored them. They are conversational units. They give us something coherent to say when a particular topic comes up in conversation. Accordingly, they do not need to have logical interconnections between them, and they are notoriously invulnerable to argument because of their isolated, molecular character. I suspect that the majority of our knowledge comes packed in little opinion molecules like these, just waiting for the topic to come up.

In conclusion: (1) It's a fact that there is more nonconsistency in heaven and earth than is dreamt of in our psychological theories; (2) I feel that the "opinion molecule" theory applies even to intellectuals—more often than they would like to think; and (3) I'm not ashamed to say so because I know Robert Abelson feels the same way.

THE EMOTIONAL FOUNDATIONS OF BELIEFS AND ATTITUDES

So far, our exploration of beliefs and attitudes has been largely confined to the area above the neck. Beliefs and attitudes, it has been implied, are to be found in the brain. But our intuitions tell us that our stronger opinions seem to have roots extending into lower regions as well. At least, the Republicans for Goldwater thought so in 1964, when they proclaimed from platform and poster that "in your heart you know he's right!" So too thought partisan wags of other persuasion who hastened to add "but in your guts you know he's nuts!" And then there are those enviable public figures who possess "charisma," a substance which presumably influences our vote through more exotic, but as yet undiscovered, organs.

There is some truth in these observations, for emotions do play an important role in beliefs and attitudes. When we are emotional for any reason, a number of physiological changes take place in our bodies. Our heart rate and blood pressure change; we perspire more freely; our digestive processes slow down; the pupils of our eyes dilate; and so forth. Both positive and negative emotions can be accompanied by such changes; and even when an emotion is so weak that the individual himself is not aware of it, sensitive measuring instruments can often detect the internal responses of the emotion. For example, the so-called lie detector is simply a collection of instruments for measuring the slight physiological changes that accompany the mild anxiety or guilt that lying may produce. It does not tell an interrogator directly whether or not a man is lying, since any upsurge in emotion (even happiness or sexual arousal) can jiggle the recording pens. The conclusion that a man has lied is only the interrogator's inference from the pattern of the physiological responses made to a carefully composed sequence of questions.

The emotional components of both positive and negative attitudes can also be detected in this same way. For example, Hess, Seltzer, and Shlien (1965) conducted a study in which pictures of men and women "pinups" were shown to both heterosexual and homosexual males. When heterosexual males looked at the female pinups, the pupils of their eyes dilated more than when they looked at the male pinups; the opposite was true for the homosexual males. In this experiment the dilation of the pupils indicated the presumably positive attitude of sexual attraction, and mild sexual arousal was probably part of the total emotional response evoked by the pictures. The emotional components of negative attitudes have also been detected physiologically. In one such experiment, the subjects were known to be either prejudiced or unprejudiced against Negroes (Porier & Lott, 1967). The study was disguised as a routine experiment which required the subject to be connected to physiological measuring equipment. One of the instruments measured the subject's galvanic skin response (GSR), a common index of emotionality which detects changes in the resistance of the skin to the passage of a very weak electrical current. In the course of the experiment, a Negro research assistant was instructed to adjust the electrodes and to "inadvertently" touch the subject as he did so. Prejudiced subjects showed greater physiological responses (GSR's) when they were touched than did unprejudiced subjects. The experiment further showed that the prejudiced subjects were not merely reacting to being touched but to being touched by a Negro.

In the Porier and Lott experiment, prejudiced subjects were actually confronted with the object of their prejudice, but a related experiment by Cooper (1959) demonstrated that the emotional components of an attitude can be present even if the actual object of the attitude is not. The attitudes of subjects in Cooper's study were either favorable or unfavorable toward a number of ethnic groups. Each subject's GSR was measured as the experimenter read aloud a number of complimentary or derogatory statements about the various ethnic groups. Stronger emotional reactions occurred whenever complimentary statements were made about disliked ethnic groups or derogatory statements were made about favored groups than when the same statements were made about more neutral groups.

Emotional reactions like these are made, not born, and it is important to discover how the links between emotions and objects are forged. How do we acquire emotional responses to particular objects and persons and even to verbal statements about those objects and persons? Two processes appear to provide the answer: classical conditioning and semantic generalization.

THE ACQUISITION OF EMOTIONAL RESPONSES: CLASSICAL CONDITIONING

The process of classical or Pavlovian conditioning was first investigated intensively by the Russian physiologist Ivan Pavlov (1849–1936). In this procedure a stimulus, called the unconditioned stimulus, is selected which automatically elicits some physiological response. For example, Pavlov used meat powder as the unconditioned stimulus because it automatically elicits salivation when placed in the mouths of dogs. He then demonstrated that any arbitrary stimulus, such as the beat of a metronome, could be given the power to elicit salivation if it was presented simultaneously or just prior to the presentation of the meat powder. That is, after several paired presentations of both the metronome beat and the meat powder, the sound of the metronome alone was sufficient to elicit salivation. The arbitrary stimulus, in this case the metronome beat, is called the conditioned stimulus.[1]

Humans, too, are susceptible to classical conditioning. For example, when the human body is exposed to cold, one of the automatic physiological reactions is the constriction of the small blood vessels near the body surface. Menzies (1937) was able to condition this response to the sound of a buzzer by sounding it at the same time the subject's hand was immersed in a container of ice water. After several pairings of cold water and buzzer, the buzzer alone was able to produce the vasoconstriction. Recent research, particularly research done in the Soviet Union, has indicated that many responses of our internal organs and nearly all the physiological indices of emotion can be conditioned through variations of the basic classical conditioning procedure.

The relevance of classical conditioning to human behavior becomes more apparent when we realize that words and even thoughts can become conditioned stimuli capable of eliciting internal emotional responses in an individual. This was shown experimentally by Roessler and Brogden (1943), who changed the ice water experiment described above by eliminating the buzzer and simply substituting a word which the experimenter said aloud as he plunged the subject's hand into the ice water. Eventually the word alone came to elicit the vasoconstriction.

The operation of a lie detector is based upon the fact that emotional responses can be classically conditioned to words and thoughts. Whenever we lied as children, we were punished, and this punishment automatically elicited all the negative physiological responses associated with anxiety and guilt. By the time we have become adults, lying has become a conditioned stimulus capable of eliciting the same physiological responses even when the original unconditioned stimuli of punishment are not present. These conditioned responses to lying are what the "lie detector" detects.

We are all familiar with an even more common example of classical conditioning: "dirty" words. We all know people (perhaps yourself) for whom these words elicit such strong emotional responses that they cannot bring themselves to say them aloud, even in private. Or if they do say them, they blush, another classically conditioned response with

---

[1]For further discussion, see Walker, *Conditioning and Instrumental Learning*, 1967, in this series.

which we are all familiar. Such words have acquired their eliciting power as conditioned stimuli because, like lying, they bring punishment in our culture.

THE TRANSMISSION OF EMOTIONAL RESPONSES: SEMANTIC GENERALIZATION

Classical conditioning by itself does not explain how the emotional components of beliefs and attitudes are created. It seems unlikely, for example, that everyone who dislikes Negroes in our society has undergone a conditioning procedure in which a Negro became the conditioned stimulus by being paired with electric shock or some other aversive unconditioned stimulus. In fact, many prejudiced individuals have never even encountered the objects of their prejudice; and, as we saw above, prejudiced individuals can have emotional responses just to complimentary verbal statements about disliked ethnic groups. It appears, then, that when we pick up the verbal or cognitive components of beliefs and attitudes, we must somehow be "catching" the emotional reactions as well. And if the emotional reactions are "contagious" in this way, then language must somehow be the transmitting medium. This is, in fact, the case, and the process underlying it is called *semantic generalization.*

When a response has been classically conditioned to some stimulus, other similar stimuli will also evoke the same response. For example, Hovland (1937) conditioned the galvanic skin response (GSR) of human subjects to an auditory tone of a particular pitch, using a mild electric shock as the unconditioned stimulus. He then found that tones of higher and lower pitch could also elicit the GSR; the further the pitch was from the original one, the less the response. This phenomenon is called *generalization* and occurs automatically whenever a response is classically conditioned. The most interesting point for our purposes, however, is that humans show generalization to stimuli which are similar to the conditioned stimulus not just in physical characteristics, but in meaning. For example, with human subjects a GSR conditioned to the *sound* of a bell may also be elicited by the *sight* of a bell or by the spoken word "bell." If conditioned to the word "bell," human subjects will generalize to the word "gong." This is the kind of generalization that is called semantic generalization. By means of it, emotional responses can generalize from objects to words, from words to objects, and from words to other words with similar meanings. It is the crucial process by which classical conditioning can create the emotional components of beliefs and attitudes.

The connection between semantic generalization and attitudes is nicely illustrated in an experiment conducted by the Soviet psychologist

Volkova (1953). She conditioned salivation in children to the Russian word for "good" by using cranberry puree as the unconditioned stimulus. The puree was delivered to the subject's mouth via a chute as the experimenter said "good" aloud. After a few trials, the word "good" by itself began to elicit the salivation. "Good" had become a conditioned stimulus. Then Volkova demonstrated that sentences like "The young pioneer helps his comrade" also produced salivation, whereas sentences like "The fascists destroyed many cities" did not.

Thus, in her experiment, Volkova first caused the word "good" to become a conditioned stimulus and then demonstrated that "good" attitude statements simultaneously acquired the power to elicit salivation. The response had generalized from one verbal stimulus ("good") to others along a dimension of common meaning. This is what we mean by semantic generalization, the transmission of a conditioned response through the medium of language.

Volkova's experiment provides a basis for suggesting that we can pick up emotional components of a prejudice through purely verbal means without ever having come into contact with the objects of the prejudice. The social environment can, in effect, perform Volkova's experiment by using words and phrases that already carry emotional connotations for us from previous conditioning experiences; these words and phrases have already become conditioned stimuli. When they are used to describe and characterize members of ethnic minorities, they transfer their emotional responses along with their meanings.

Two psychologists, Arthur and Carolyn Staats (1958), checked this hypothesis more directly by working with the names of six nationalities: German, Swedish, Italian, French, Dutch, and Greek. Subjects in their experiment were told that they were to learn lists of words. In the critical "conditioning" phase of the experiment, each nationality name was presented visually followed by some other word. Each nationality name was presented 18 times in random order. For one group of subjects, the word Dutch was always followed by a word with a positive evaluative meaning (e.g., pretty, sweet, gift, healthy), and the word Swedish was followed by a word with a negative evaluative meaning (e.g., bitter, ugly, failure). This was reversed for a second group: Swedish was followed by positive words and Dutch by negative words. The other nationality names were always followed by neutral words (e.g., chair, with, twelve). Thus, Dutch and Swedish played the role of conditioned stimuli, and the positive and negative words were the unconditioned stimuli (since they presumably already had the power to elicit emotional reactions).

At the end of the experiment, each subject rated how he felt about each nationality name on a set of seven-point scales. For example, he was asked to rate *German* on a seven-point scale ranging from "unpleasant" to "pleasant." (The results from subjects who became aware that the experimenters were trying to condition them were not included in the final analysis.) The results supported the hypothesis of the experiment: the group that had heard favorable words in conjunction with *Dutch* rated it as very pleasant, good, etc., whereas they expressed negative feelings about *Swedish* on the same scales. As predicted, the ratings for the other group were reversed. Although it is still a logical leap from the results of this study to the conclusion that ethnic-group prejudice is formed by an analogous process, I am willing to conclude that classical conditioning and semantic generalization do play such a role in establishing some of the emotional components of prejudice.

THE ELIMINATION OF EMOTIONAL RESPONSES: EXTINCTION

As a practical matter, eliminating the emotional components of beliefs and attitudes is often of more concern than creating them. Therapists often seek to remove the anxiety or other emotional reactions of their clients, and social psychologists are sometimes called upon to recommend strategies for decreasing antagonistic racial feelings. Obviously these are complex tasks that involve more than just physiological reactions, but such reactions are still part of the total belief or attitude that must be directly or indirectly modified. One direct procedure for modifying emotional reactions experimentally is called extinction, a procedure first analyzed intensively by Pavlov.

After conditioning has been established, extinction of the conditioned response can be effected by presenting the conditioned stimulus repeatedly without pairing it with the unconditioned stimulus. If dogs have been conditioned to salivate at the sound of a buzzer by using meat powder as the unconditioned stimulus, repeated presentation of the buzzer without the meat powder will cause the amount of salivation to decrease on each trial until the buzzer no longer has any measurable effect. Although the procedure is fairly straightforward, its theoretical explanation is still a matter of controversy.[2] Most psychologists believe that extinction is not a mere passive disappearance of the emotional response, but is instead an active inhibition of the response or an active process of learning some alternative response which interferes with the conditioned response.

You are already acquainted with the extinction phenomenon in the case of "dirty" words. If we use them frequently, our emotional responses to them extinguish, and the words begin to sound neutral to us.

[2] See Walker, *Conditioning and Instrumental Learning*, pp. 67–76.

The phenomenon of extinction thus suggests a sound psychological—as opposed to moral—argument against the free and excessive use of profanity and obscenity in our daily conversation. If we use such terms too frequently, we deplete our vocabularies of words with emotional punch; our language becomes so emotionally flattened that nothing is on tap for the ripe occasion when we yearn for some eliciting power. Similarly, since our internal physiology ceases to "tell" us that the words are "nasty," we can easily forget that they still elicit emotional reactions in others. You have probably heard the apocryphal story about the soldier home on leave who startles his family with a bland "Please pass the f_____g butter."

Temporary extinction, called adaptation, also occurs over short intervals of time. For example, when reading a modern novel, we adapt to the taboo words after a while and display little or no emotional response to them, but our emotional reactions reappear when the same words are used in a different context. Imagine, for example, how your internal physiology might have jumped a few seconds ago if the publisher had not overruled me and deleted the taboo word in the previous paragraph.

And even though I strongly object to this bit of silly censorship, I must admit that it provides an elegant example of the very point I am making: the deletion reflects the publisher's fear that such taboo words—to which you have probably adapted in works of fiction—might be "offensive" in the context of a book like this. When and if our classically conditioned responses to taboo words extinguish further, so will the publisher's classically conditioned sensitivity to those responses.

Over time the emotional meanings to words change in ways that parallel changing beliefs and attitudes toward the concepts associated with those words. Conditioning, extinction, and reconditioning take place through the medium of mediated generalization. The recent history of synonyms for the word "Negro" provides an excellent example. Almost all of us, except overt bigots, have strong negative reactions to the word "nigger." Over the years, some of the older Southern politicians have switched from "nigger" to "nigra" in their public utterances, and they switch to "Negro" as soon as they begin to hunt for national constituencies. If you are over 35 (black or white) and reasonably conservative, you are probably still emotionally comfortable with the adjective "colored," but the term "black" probably bothers you just as much as if it were a variant of "nigger." On the other hand, if you are under 35 or are sympathetic to the newer militant mood, "black" is indeed beautiful, whereas "colored" elicits all the disgust associated with the past ("Them colored folk sure do like watermelon"). No civil rights organization founded today would ever call itself the "National Association for the

Advancement of Colored People." As you probably know, the emotional connotations of "Negro" are currently undergoing the same transformation as "colored." The word remains fairly neutral in formal or technical writing ("The Negro research assistant was instructed to touch the subject . . ." "White attitudes toward the Negro showed a 20% change . . ."), but in discussions specifically related to the racial issue, it has acquired negative connotations, and the term "black" is more popular. Only "black" retains some of the emotional bite and sharpness appropriate to the new militancy.

EXTINCTION THERAPY

The extinction and reconditioning processes described above are essentially unplanned; they occur as accompaniments to changes in related beliefs and attitudes. But scientific findings are often put to direct and deliberate use, and the phenomenon of extinction is no exception. For example, a new school of psychotherapy has emerged which attempts to remove negative emotional responses to objects and situations through extinction procedures. (These are sometimes called counter-conditioning procedures since extinction is often viewed as the learning of an alternative response which displaces the conditioned response.) The patient is first taught deep relaxation techniques; he is then asked to picture a series of situations, éach one resembling more closely than the previous one the real situation to which he has an aversion. He practices the relaxation responses as each successive stimulus situation is imagined until he is able to relax (show no anxiety) to the thought of the actual situation he fears. Proponents of this method of therapy claim that it extinguishes or inhibits the negative emotional responses of the patient when he is actually placed in the situation he has previously shunned, and their published reports support this assertion. Some critics, however, have questioned the theoretical claim that the techniques are really analogous to extinction procedures in the laboratory. They object to the fact that the patient is merely asked to imagine the situation he fears rather than actually being confronted with the real stimulus situation. It may be, however, that such procedures are analogous to laboratory extinction procedures and that the ability of the patient to transfer his physiological relaxation from the imagined to the real situation is a reflection of semantic generalization. The controversy is still a lively one in the field. (See, for example, Breger & McGaugh, 1965, 1966; Rachman & Eysenck, 1966.)

UNINTENTIONAL EXTINCTION THERAPY

We should not jump to the conclusion that it is always desirable to extinguish negative emotional responses to aversive situations. Most of us, for example, feel a certain amount of anxiety and revulsion toward brutality and violence, and it is precisely this revulsion which motivates us to suppress brutality and violence in our society. In other words, such emotional reactions are one of the psychological mechanisms upon which society relies for controlling violence. Until society can devise more effective ways of controlling violence, it is probably premature to tranquilize our feelings of revulsion toward it.

Thus, there is a sound psychological reason for objecting to the unnecessary display of violence in films and on television. Because such violence is not actually paired with pain for us viewers, a circumstance which would condition us to dislike violence all the more, our conditioned emotional responses gradually extinguish; our tolerance for violence increases. It seems reasonable to suppose that as our collective tolerance increases, public opposition to displays of violence diminishes, permitting the media to introduce even more graphic materials and, in effect, to initiate a new round of "extinction therapy." In fact, this process seems apparent to me in television news broadcasts of Vietnam battle scenes. The networks remove any material which is too objectionable to the public (that is, material which might maintain our emotional revulsion against violence) but they retain as much of the visual horror as we can "comfortably" tolerate. You will recognize that this is precisely how an extinction therapist would proceed if he wanted to enable his patient to put up with an ever-increasing amount of violence in his environment. Perhaps, as a society, we should conclude that until alternative controls are available the social costs of having us "well adjusted" are too high.

But this argument cuts two ways. If we propose to censor the mass media on the grounds that we don't want to eliminate the negative emotional reactions people have to violence and brutality, how do we respond to those who, like my aunt, propose to censor scenes of lovemaking and nudity on the same grounds? As it happens, I don't like violence and brutality. I do like lovemaking and nudity. Therefore, I favor retaining negative emotional reactions to the first two and removing negative emotional reactions to the last two. Perhaps you agree. But these value judgments do not themselves derive from the principle of extinction—or from any other scientific principle, for that matter. Such principles can be used to support either side of the censorship argument; they are available free of charge not only to the life-loving innocents among us, but to my aunt, the dean of women, and the district attorney as well.

THE SELF-PERCEPTION OF EMOTIONAL RESPONSES

Let's suppose that it's true: In our heart we know we're right. The question is how do we know what's in our heart? How do we know what we feel about something? This question is rarely asked because the answer seems so obvious: we just do! That is, we assume that we have direct and unerring knowledge of all our internal states, including our beliefs and attitudes. This is, of course, just another way of saying that most of our beliefs about our own internal states are first-order primitive beliefs. They would seem to require no justification beyond a citation of direct experience which, in this case, includes internal as well as external experience. We hold a nonconscious zero-order faith in the credibility of our "internal" sense that is comparable in every way to our implicit trust in the credibility of our sensory experiences of the outside world.

But we should be more cautious. When it comes to inner knowledge, our implicit trust is not always justified, and we are far less capable of recognizing and labeling inner states than we imagine. We can maintain our naive faith and not be forced to confront our incompetence in this regard only because people know better than to call upon us to make internal identifications which we have not been explicitly trained to make. ("Is it your spleen or your liver which is tingling, Mrs. Jones?") It is my view that, with very few exceptions, internal identifications that we have not been taught remain internal identifications that we cannot make. Self-knowledge, I shall argue, comes to us from without. Let us see why.

THE ORIGINS OF SELF-PERCEPTION

In order to identify and name things in his environment, a child must initially have someone else around to help him, someone who will play the game of "pointing and naming," who will teach the child to distinguish between objects and events that appear similar and to label them with different descriptions. The problem, which does not occur to most people as a problem, is to understand how it is that a child learns to identify and describe his internal states and feelings to which nobody else has access.

Part of the answer is "metaphor." That is, occasionally a child will be able to label some internal event automatically by using a metaphor borrowed from a description of the outside world. "Butterflies in the stomach" is a common example, and I have heard of one child who described the prickly sensation in a foot which had "fallen asleep" as feeling like "ginger ale when I hold the glass to my face." But the cases in which metaphors can be used are exceptions. Most of the time, the child must be explicitly taught how to describe his internal states in the same way he is taught to describe his outer environment: someone must be able to "point and name." And here's the rub, for mommy and daddy do not have direct access to the inner world they are teaching the child to describe, and hence, they must resort to a kind of guesswork. For example, the first time they teach the child to know that his head is "hurting," they must be sure that his head is, in fact, hurting rather than that his scalp is itching or his foot throbbing. And since they do not have direct access to such private happenings, they must inevitably base their knowledge of the child's internal states on publicly observable cues. They must see the child bump his head, cry, or display a wound, for example. But whatever cues they use must necessarily be outside, not inside, the child. As one precocious 5-year-old put it to his mother (who kept asking him how he was feeling after the external signs of an allergic reaction had disappeared): "Don't you wish you could be inside of me? Then you would *know* how I was feeling, because now you can only ask me, and I can be wrong or I might lie to you and you'd never know."[3]

The fact that others must teach us to describe our internal perceptions on the basis of external cues has even given rise to philosophical problems. For example, consider the hypothetical case of an individual who is "miswired" so that he sees blue whenever anyone else sees yellow and vice versa. Such a person would always apply the words "blue" and "yellow" in the "correct" ways—that is, in the ways appropriate to the external cues—because others used those cues to teach him which words to use in the first place. As a result, there is no way in which he or anyone else could ever discover the discrepancy. (You may have to think about that for a while, but it's true. You may even be such an individual!)

Thus, we have learned to identify many of our internal states only because outside observers first inferred those states from observable external cues and then taught us how to label the internal situation that they assumed was accompanying those cues. Injury—pain—tears; external cause—internal state—external effect. These are the correlations upon which individual A's knowledge of individual B's internal states is based. These are, therefore, the correlations upon which individual B's knowledge of his own internal states is based.

THE SELF-PERCEPTION HYPOTHESIS

These considerations lead us to the major hypothesis of this section: *In identifying his own internal states, an individual partially relies on the same external cues that others use when they infer his internal states.*

In other words, we may think that we are always reading our internal states directly, but we "cheat" and peek outside to look at the same clues that others look at when they want to know our internal states. Furthermore, we are usually unaware that we do so. Let us look at some evidence for this hypothesis.

---

[3]The child is Adam Zimbardo, who, his psychologist father assures me, discovered this fact of self-perception on his own. (But I published first, Adam.)

One of the most famous of the experiments which can be interpreted in this way was conducted by Stanley Schachter and Jerome Singer (1962). In this experiment, subjects were injected with a drug similar to adrenalin, a drug which speeds up the heart, causes perspiration, changes the breathing, and, generally, provokes the internal physiological reactions that accompany strong emotions. The subjects, however, were not informed of the true effects of the injection. They were placed in a waiting room with a confederate of the experimenter while the drug took effect. The confederate pretended to be another subject who was going through the experiment; and for some of the subjects he pretended to be very angry. He muttered about a questionnaire they had been given to fill out, grumbled out loud about the experiment, and finally threw his questionnaire into a wastebasket and stomped out. For other subjects, the confederate pretended to be very happy, played "basketball" with wads of paper and the wastebasket, twirled a hula hoop, and tried to get the subject to join in the fun. Following these sessions with the confederate, all subjects were asked to assess their own emotional moods. Schachter and Singer were interested in discovering how the combination of internal and external cues would affect the subject's perceptions of his own emotionality. The experiment was also repeated with subjects who had not been given the drug but had been given a placebo injection of saline solution, which has no effect on internal physiological reactions.

The results showed that subjects who had been injected with the placebo perceived themselves to be relatively unemotional after the session with the confederate regardless of how the confederate had behaved. But subjects who had been injected with the drug felt quite different. Those who had been with the angry confederate described their own mood as one of anger; those who had been with the happy confederate felt slightly "euphoric" and happy. In other words, Schachter and Singer demonstrated that they could evoke self-descriptions of emotional states as disparate as anger and euphoria from subjects in whom identical states of physiological arousal had been induced. The subjects clearly needed the internal cues provided by the drug to identify the fact that they were in an emotional state, but the more subtle discrimination of *which* emotion they were experiencing was dependent upon the external cues of the situation—that is, upon the behavior of the confederate.

Finally, Schachter and Singer report that even drugged subjects did not describe themselves as emotional if they knew ahead of time what reactions to expect from the drug. These subjects had an alternative explanation—the drug—for the internal cues they experienced and hence did not interpret their internal states as emotions. Again we see that cues from our external environment weigh heavily in determining how we perceive and interpret our internal states.

Evidence for the external-cue hypothesis of self-perception can also be found in situations less exotic than the experimental laboratory. For example, Schachter (1968) has suggested that overweight individuals may eat too much or too often because they do not rely upon internal stomach cues to tell themselves that they are hungry, but instead rely primarily upon external circumstances. Schachter and one of his colleagues (Schachter & Gross, 1968) obtained evidence for this suggestion in a clever study in which both obese and normal subjects were required to sit quietly in a room for 30 minutes with nothing to do. The room contained a clock which was rigged to run fast for some subjects and slow for others. The experimenter left the room when the clock read 5:05 P.M. When he returned a half hour later, the clock read 6:05 for some subjects but only 5:20 for others. Each subject was then allowed to have a snack from a box of crackers. The box of crackers was later weighed to see how much the subject had eaten.

The results showed that obese subjects ate more crackers when the clock read 6:05 than they did when it only read 5:20. In other words, obese subjects utilized the apparent time of day (about dinner time) as the cue to tell them how hungry they were. Normal subjects did not do this. (In fact, normal-weight subjects actually ate fewer crackers when the clock read 6:05; a few of them commented that they didn't want to spoil their appetites for dinner!)

If obese individuals really do rely less upon internal cues than normal individuals, as this study suggests, then they should actually be *better* able to tolerate food deprivation than normal individuals if the external cues are removed. Schachter and his colleagues also thought of this possibility (Goldman, Jaffa, & Schachter, 1968). They discovered in their study that obese Jews were more likely to fast on Yom Kippur, the Jewish Day of Atonement, than were normal-weight Jews. Furthermore, the more time obese Jews spent in the synagogue (away from external food cues), the easier it was for them to fast. The normal-weight Jews, on the other hand, carried their (internal) hunger cues into the synagogue with them. For them, being in the synagogue had little to do with the difficulty of the fast.

If we move from the synagogue to more subversive environs, such as the college campus, we can find still more instances in which our ability to identify internal stimulation cannot be taken for granted. Marijuana smokers, for example, often claim that they had to "learn" what internal reactions constituted the "high," and even if they knew immediately they had to learn to regard such sensations as pleasant. They also report that a large part of the perceived internal experience produced by marijuana continues to be strongly influenced by the external social situation in which it is used. Finally, those adventurous souls who are willing to risk the possible medical consequences of using LSD to explore inner space tell us that their private "trips" are literally indescribable. Such an admission (boast?) may well be a tribute to the novelty of the LSD experience, but in itself it hardly constitutes persuasive evidence for a new process of obtaining insightful self-knowledge.

I am a romantic at heart, but, in the head, a psychologist. In the final analysis, most self-knowledge must still come to us from without, even if a drug helps us process it differently once it is inside.

We have been considering the self-perception of internal states in general, and we should expect the self-perception of attitudes to follow the same rules. We should find that an individual's perception of his own attitudes can also be led astray if misleading external cues are introduced. A clever demonstration of this has been provided by Stuart Valins (1966). Valins conducted an experiment in which male subjects were shown slides of seminude women. The subjects believed that the experimenter was measuring their physiological reactions to the pictures, and they could hear what they thought was their heartbeat coming from a tape recorder hooked up to the measuring apparatus. Actually, however, a false heartbeat had been prerecorded and was being piped through the recorder. The recording was set so that they would hear the heartbeat change markedly when some of the pictures were shown on the screen. After the experiment, each subject was asked to rate how well he liked each of the pictures he had seen, and he was permitted to choose some of them to take home.

Valins reports that pictures on which the heartbeat either increased or decreased markedly were rated as significantly more attractive by the subjects than those on which no heartbeat change had occurred, and the subjects chose more of these "more attractive" pictures to take home. Even four to five weeks after the experiment, subjects still preferred these pictures. One interpretation of this result is that the subjects based their attitudes toward the pictures upon what they thought were their internal reactions to them, whereas, in fact, the "internal reactions" were external and had been predetermined. The external heartbeat cues overrode any internal cues upon which they might otherwise have based their attitudes.

The supporters of Barry Goldwater's 1964 bid for the presidency who assured us that "in your heart you know he's right" should take some consolation from these findings. In our hearts we may well have known. But those external cues were all so confusing!

THE BEHAVIORAL FOUNDATIONS OF BELIEFS AND ATTITUDES

If we were to ask a friend, "Why do you eat brown bread?" we would not consider it unusual if he replied, "Because I like it." Such an answer would be satisfactory because we readily accept the idea that an attitude (liking) can cause a behavior (eating). This is, in fact, the prevailing view in our society: Attitudes cause behavior. This view underlies the frequent suggestion that the only effective way to end racism is to "change the hearts and minds of men." Thus, it is argued, legislation against racial discrimination will be ineffective because it will not be able to bring about the necessary attitude change: "State-ways cannot change folkways."

But the theme of this chapter is just the opposite: Behavior causes attitudes. That is, there is now sufficient evidence to suggest that, under certain conditions, one of the most effective ways to "change the hearts and minds of men" is to change their behavior. In fact, this may even be easier than the other way around. Conventional wisdom suggests that good-will campaigns and brotherhood weeks may convince people to discriminate less, but there is better evidence that suggests making people discriminate less may convince them to have good will and act like brothers. To see how behavior might serve as a foundation for beliefs and attitudes, we shall look at two theories: the theory of cognitive dissonance (Festinger, 1957) and the self-perception theory, which I introduced in Chapter 5 of this book.

Most people agree that the question, "Why do you eat brown bread?" can properly be answered with "Because I like it." I should like to convince you, however, that the question, "Why do you like brown bread?" frequently ought to be answered with "Because I eat it."

THE THEORY OF COGNITIVE DISSONANCE

Leon Festinger's theory of cognitive dissonance has been the most influential of the cognitive consistency theories. I have purposely postponed discussion of this theory until now because it is the only consistency theory which deals explicitly with the consistencies and inconsistencies between an individual's behavior and his beliefs or attitudes. In fact, most of the recent experimental evidence for the hypothesis that behavior causes attitudes has come from the testing of this theory.

Festinger's theory postulates, among other things, that if an individual is induced to engage in behavior that is inconsistent with his beliefs or attitudes, he will experience the discomfort of "cognitive dissonance," which will motivate him to seek a resolution of that inconsistency. One way he can do this is to convince himself that he actually believes in what he has done, that he actually holds the beliefs or attitudes implied by his behavior. In other words, the inconsistency, or "dissonance," between an individual's beliefs or attitudes and his behavior will motivate belief or attitude change toward cognitive consistency. This is, of course, just a variation of the basic cognitive consistency hypothesis which I discussed at length in Chapter 4.

A psychologist at Yale, Arthur Cohen, decided to test the theory by taking advantage of an incident which took place on the campus in the spring of 1959 (Brehm & Cohen, 1962, pp. 73–77). There had been a student "riot" on the campus, the New Haven police had intervened, and accusations of police brutality soon followed. The issue was a very bitter one, and most of the student body felt that the police actions were quite unjustified. For his experiment, Cohen and a class of his students went around the campus and selected students one at a time at random and asked them to write a strong, forceful essay entitled "Why the New Haven Police Actions Were Justified," an essay which was to argue in favor of the police side of the riots. To some of these students, the experimenters offered $10; to others, $5; to others, $1; and to a final group, 50¢. Thus, each student was offered a predetermined sum of money for writing the essay, and subtle pressure was applied until he agreed to comply. After writing his essay, the student indicated his actual opinion of the police actions on a questionnaire. This same questionnaire was used to survey the opinions of a control group, a group of students selected at random who had not been asked to write essays. Cohen was interested in discovering whether or not writing the essays caused the students to persuade themselves of their arguments—that is, to become more favorable toward the police actions. He was further interested in discovering whether the amount of money used to induce the student to write the essay made any difference in the amount of self-persuasion that took place.

The results showed that students who had written the essays for either $10 or $5 subsequently expressed opinions which did not differ significantly from the opinions expressed by the control group of students who had not been asked to write essays. That is, writing the essays, even for relatively large sums of money, had not persuaded them; they still felt the police had been quite unjustified. But the interesting finding was that subjects who had been paid only $1 to write essays did become significantly more favorable toward the police actions as a result of writing their essays. Students who were paid only 50¢ for their essays became even more favorable toward the police than the $1 subjects. In other words, the *less* the individual was paid to engage in the "dissonant" behavior of writing the essay, the *more* he persuaded himself to believe what he had written!

These results may seem quite surprising, maybe even the opposite of what you had anticipated, but they are exactly what the theory of cognitive dissonance predicts. According to the theory, writing the essay should produce inconsistency because, given the individual's initial attitudes, there is "no good reason" why he should be writing such an essay. But the large sum of money removes that inconsistency for him by giving him a very good reason for writing the essay. He can now justify the behavior to himself, and, accordingly, there is no longer any "dissonance pressure" upon him to bring his attitudes into line with his behavior. There is no longer any conflict between engaging in pro-police behavior and at the same time retaining an anti-police attitude. On the other hand, writing the essay for little or no compensation does not provide the individual with a "good reason" for his behavior; so he finds no convenient rationalization (such as money). Accordingly, he will suffer from the pressure of dissonance, or inconsistency, until he changes his opinions to make them consistent with his behavior. He will become more favorable toward the police. In other words, the theory predicts that the smaller the compensation, the greater the dissonance, and therefore the greater the attitude change. These are the results of Cohen's Yale experiment.

This same pattern of results has also been obtained in other experiments using different procedures and inducements, and other predictions made by the theory concerning the "behavior causes attitudes" sequence have also been confirmed. In general, Festinger's theory of cognitive dissonance has had a pretty good batting average, and the unintuitive nature of many of its predictions has brought it widespread attention.

Dissonance theory has also been criticized, however (e.g., Chapanis & Chapanis, 1964). One of the difficulties has been that dissonance theory experiments are rather complicated, and their results are open to other interpretations. That is, the experiments often support the theory, but they are also consistent with other theoretical ways of looking at the results. I myself am involved in just such a controversy with some of the dissonance theorists, and we shall reconsider the Yale experiment on my own theoretical territory in the next section.[1]

---

[1]If you are interested in the controversy itself, see Bem (1965, 1967a, 1967b, 1968); Bem & McConnell (1970); Elms (1967); Jones, Linder, Kiesler, Zanna & Brehm (1968); Kiesler, Nisbett, & Zanna (1969); Mills (1967); and Piliavin, Piliavin, Loewenton, McCauley, & Hammond (1969).

SELF-PERCEPTION THEORY

My theory of self-perception also predicts that attitudes should follow behavior. You will recall that in Chapter 5 I noted that individual A infers that individual B is experiencing some internal state by relying on publicly observable external cues. I attempted to argue from that fact that individual B also relies on some of these same external cues to inform himself of what emotion he is experiencing and what attitudes he holds. In the experiments and examples discussed, the external cues were found to reside in the social or physical situation in which the individual was placed. But that is not the only source of such cues. To us, as observers, the most important clues to an individual's inner states are found in his behavior. When we want to know how a person feels, we look to see how he acts. Accordingly, my theory about the origins of an individual's self-knowledge predicts that he might also infer his own internal states by observing his own overt behavior. Such is, in fact, the case.

Suppose that we observe an individual receiving a series of electric shocks to his hand. Furthermore, suppose that we know he can choose to push a button to terminate the shock, or he can choose to endure the shock for two seconds until it terminates automatically. On one shock, we see him push the button; on another, we see that he does not. All other things being equal, we would infer that the shock he chose to terminate must have been more painful or uncomfortable than the shock he chose to endure. That is, we use his behavior as our guide to infer his state of discomfort. The question is: Will the individual himself also use his behavior as a guide to infer the discomfort of the shock? To test this possibility, two of my students and I (Bandler, Madaras, & Bem, 1968) paid volunteer subjects to undergo a series of electric shocks. The subjects were not told that all the shocks were of equal intensity. Prior to each shock, we told the subject whether we preferred him to escape it or to endure it but that the final choice was his. In this way we were, in fact, able to control which shocks the subject terminated and which they endured, even though they saw themselves as having a choice in the matter. After each shock, the subject rated the degree of discomfort from it on a 7-point scale.

The results supported the self-perception theory. Our subjects rated the shocks as significantly more uncomfortable when they escaped them than they did when they endured them, the same inference an outside observer would have drawn. This was true even though the endured shocks were necessarily longer than the escaped shocks. We also found that the subject had to believe he had a choice of enduring or escaping; if we told him to push the escape button so that we could "measure his reaction time" when the shock came on, then he did not use his behavior as a guide for inferring the discomfort of the shock. This too is the same inference an outside observer would make: if he saw the subject pushing the button only because the experimenter required it, he could not use the subject's behavior as a basis for inferring the degree of discomfort the shock had produced.

We have always known that individual A tries to infer the internal states of individual B by observing B's behavior. We now see that individual B looks at his own behavior to help him infer his own inner states. This is, of course, just a special case of the self-perception hypothesis discussed in Chapter 5. Now let us apply this hypothesis to the perception of beliefs and attitudes.

First, consider how we, as outside observers, infer the beliefs and attitudes of others. Consider, for example, our reactions to some well-known figure who personally endorses a product in a television commercial. What do we conclude about his real, private attitudes? Usually we take his endorsement with a grain of salt because we know he is being paid. That is, we are usually inclined to attribute his enthusiasm to cash rather than conviction. We assume that his behavior has nothing to do with his own private attitudes toward the product. However, Madison Avenue has moved to still our cynical scoffs and stifle our stubborn skepticism by resorting to the "candid camera" technique. In these commercials, some barely articulate housewives or some burly construction workers are accosted in street or supermarket, where they spontaneously wax enthusiastic about Aerowax or bubble about Babo. Our inference, the advertisers hope, is that these homey folks must really prefer Brand Whatever since they have no ulterior motive (like money) for saying so. That is, since they are not being paid for their praise, their endorsements more likely reflect their actual attitudes.

This example shows that we not only use the behavior of an individual as a guide for inferring his beliefs and attitudes, but also take into account the circumstances that appear to be responsible for his behavior. We look at motives as well as behavior. In the case of a television commercial, we use the large sum of money paid to the communicator as a kind of "lie" signal, or cue, to tell us that his behavior should not be used as a basis for inferring his actual attitudes. On the other hand, a small payoff, or no payoff at all, serves as a "truth" signal; we are more inclined to take the individual's endorsement at face value and use it as a guide to his actual attitudes. In general, then, we might guess that *the smaller the sum of money paid a communicator, the more likely we are to infer that he holds the attitudes he is proclaiming in his communication.*

YALE REVISITED

We are now in a position to reinterpret the Yale experiment: Why did students who were paid the smaller sums of money come to believe the position they had advocated in their essays more than students who were paid the larger sums of money?

Perhaps you have already anticipated my interpretation of these results. If we, as observers, use the payoff to a communicator to help us judge whether or not the individual really believes what he is communicating, then it may also be that the communicator himself, as a self-observer, uses the payoff as a signal to tell *himself* whether or not his communication represents his true beliefs. In the Yale study, an individual who had been paid a large sum of money could look at his behavior, see that he was "doing it for the money," and hence perceive no connection between his behavior and his actual attitudes. His attitude would therefore be the same as that of most other students on the campus. On the other hand, an individual who had been induced to write the pro-police essay for little or no money could look at his behavior and infer from it (nonconsciously) that he must be somewhat favorable toward the police actions. ("Why else would I have written the essay?") In other words, the self-perception theory also predicts the results of the Yale study—the smaller the compensation, the more the final attitude of the essay writer will reflect the position he advocated in the essay.

To test this interpretation, I gave some students written descriptions of the situation at Yale (Bem, 1965). The descriptions mentioned that a Yale student had been asked to write an essay supporting the police actions. Some of the descriptions said the Yale student had been offered $1 to write the essay; other descriptions said the student had been offered only 50¢. These were the two sums that produced significantly changed attitudes toward the police in the Yale experiment. All my subjects were also told that the student had agreed to write the essay. After reading the descriptions given them, my subjects were asked to judge what the actual attitude of the essay writer was toward the police actions. In other words, each of my subjects acted like an outside observer. Each knew about the riot and the police actions; he knew that the Yale student had accepted a particular sum of money for writing a pro-police essay; and he was asked to use all this information to infer the actual attitude of the Yale student. Each thus had the same kind of information that the essay writer himself had about his own behavior and about the circumstances at Yale. Finally, I asked a separate group of students to estimate the attitude of a Yale student in general (one who had not been asked to write an essay).

The results of this little experiment confirmed the self-perception analysis by showing that the attitude judgments of the "observers" in my study were almost identical with the actual attitudes of Cohen's subjects; the judgments in my study showed the same inverse relationship to the amount of money offered that Cohen's study showed. In other words, in my experiment, individual A looked at individual B (the student in the Yale study) and asked himself, "What must this man's attitude be if he is willing to behave in this fashion in this situation?" Because individual A arrived at the same answer as that arrived at by individual B, we have some evidence for the self-perception hypothesis: individual B looks at his own behavior and arrives at his own attitude by implicitly and nonconsciously asking himself, "What must my attitude be if I am willing to behave in this fashion in this situation?"

A DIRECT TEST OF THE SELF-PERCEPTION HYPOTHESIS

As I noted earlier, one of the difficulties with experiments like the Yale study is that they are often too complicated to ensure that only one theory can explain them. We have already seen that the Yale study can be interpreted in at least two ways. (A psychologist named Milton Rosenberg [1965] has suggested a third.) One complication in the Yale study is that the money payoffs can have different meanings. Thus, my theory suggests that the small and large amounts of money act respectively as "truth" or "lie" signals to the individuals, telling them whether or not to believe their own essays. But money can also act as a reward for writing the essay, a possibility that has inspired some psychologists to demonstrate that under some conditions the *larger* amount of money produces the greater attitude change (Janis & Gilmore, 1965). In other words, the self-perception hypothesis that individuals sometimes infer their attitudes from their own behavior receives only indirect support from the Yale study. To obtain more direct support for the hypothesis, I conducted an experiment in which "truth" and "lie" signals were "raised from birth" in the laboratory so that their meanings would be unambiguous (Bem, 1965).

In this experiment, each subject underwent a training procedure in which he answered simple questions about himself. After each question a tape recorder was turned on, which automatically turned on a colored light. The subject was instructed to answer the question truthfully whenever the light was amber. Whenever the light was green, he was to make up a false answer to the question and say it aloud into the tape recorder. In this way, the subject learned that he could believe himself whenever he spoke in the presence of the amber light but could not believe himself in the presence of the green light. After this training session, the subject was required to state attitudes I knew he disagreed with. For example, he had to state aloud that he thought a cartoon was very funny, whereas he had indicated before the experiment that he did not think it was funny at all. The tape recorder was turned on just before he made each statement so that one of the colored lights was on while he spoke. Sometimes the "truth" light was on, sometimes the "lie" light.

Each time after the subject had made a statement and the recorder (and light) had been turned off, he was asked to indicate his true attitude on an attitude scale.

As the self-perception hypothesis predicted, the subjects changed their attitudes significantly more when they made their statements in the presence of the "truth" light than when they made their statements in the presence of the "lie" light. For example, if a subject said "This is a very funny cartoon" in the presence of the "truth" light, then he subsequently believed the cartoon to be funnier than if he had made the statement in the presence of the "lie" light. In other words, the "truth" light acted just like the small sums of money in the Yale experiment, signaling to the individual that his behavior was an indication of his true attitude; the "lie" light acted like the large sums of money, telling the individual that his behavior was irrelevant to his true attitude. Furthermore, the subjects in the two-light experiment were not aware that they had changed their attitudes as a result of their statements or the lights. As we have seen throughout this discussion of self-perception, the process of self-inference is not necessarily conscious.

INDUCING BELIEF IN FALSE CONFESSIONS

During the 1960s the United States Supreme Court rendered a series of decisions relating to the interrogation procedures of law enforcement agencies. Two of the most controversial decisions, *Escobedo* v. *Illinois* and *Miranda* v. *Arizona,* attempted to spell out in detail the safeguards that had to be extended to a prime suspect during interrogation. Under the Court-imposed guidelines, the suspect first had to be fully informed of his rights. In addition, he had the right to have an attorney present; if he could not afford an attorney, he could ask to have one provided for him; he also had the right to terminate the interrogation at any time. Finally, if he chose to waive any of these rights, the police had to obtain his written consent stating that he did so freely and without being coerced. The reasoning of the Court was (1) that the Fifth Amendment to the Constitution protects a man from having to testify against himself when on trial and (2) that if this protection is to have any substance, then it must also exist during the interrogation before the trial.

These decisions provoked a great deal of controversy concerning the balance between the rights of the individual, on the one hand, and society's right to be protected from criminals, on the other. In the summer of 1966, the Senate Subcommittee on Constitutional Amendments (a subcommittee of the Judiciary Committee) held hearings to see whether or not a constitutional amendment should be adopted to modify or nullify the Court's decisions. A number of witnesses were called to testify on various aspects of the interrogation process. As you might surmise, most of the law enforcement officials who testified tended to believe that the Court decisions had moved too far to the individual-rights side of the balance (as did Truman Capote, author of *In Cold Blood*, a novel about two murderers). The behavioral scientists who testified were, naturally enough, more sensitive to the possible psychological effects of interrogation and tended to approve the Court decisions (as did a witness from the faculty of a law school).

I was one of the behavioral scientists asked to testify before the subcommittee. Specifically, I was asked to discuss some of the possible psychological effects that the interrogation procedures might have on the beliefs and memories of the suspect himself. Could the process of interrogation itself confuse a suspect or eyewitness by clouding his memory of the events about which he is being questioned? Could an unethical interrogator lead an innocent suspect to believe in a false confession he might be induced to make? In short, when might saying become believing?[2]

It seemed to me that part of the answer to this question was provided by the Yale experiment and my laboratory experiment with the "truth" and "lie" lights. These studies suggested that saying becomes believing whenever an individual makes statements under conditions in which he expects himself to be telling the truth. Thus, it occurred to me that a man might also be confused or misled by false statements or false confessions made under "truth" conditions. To test this possibility, I conducted another experiment (Bem, 1966a) with "truth" and "lie" lights. But unlike the earlier experiment, the subjects were first required to perform some act ("crime") about which they could be questioned later. For this purpose, each subject was given a list of 100 common nouns and an alphabetical list containing 50 of those nouns. He was asked to cross out every word on the master list which also appeared on the alphabetical list. In other words, his "crime" consisted of crossing out some words and not crossing out others. Each subject then went through the preliminary training session described earlier, in which he learned to make true statements whenever the amber recording light was on and false statements whenever the green recording light was on. Then, he was required to make statements about the 100 nouns. Sometimes he was required to state aloud that he had crossed out a word and sometimes to state that he had not crossed out a word (e.g., "I did not cross out the word *tree*"). Unknown to the subject, half the statements he had to make were true, and half were false. Again, the colored lights were connected to the tape recorder so that sometimes the amber light was on as he made his "confession" and sometimes the green light. After each confession, the subject indicated on a sheet of paper whether he recalled crossing out the word or recalled not crossing it out. He also indicated how sure he was that his memory was correct. For the purpose of comparison, the subject was also asked about a number of words that had not been mentioned in his confessions.

The results of this study showed that in the presence of the "lie" light the false confessions had no effect. The subjects were able to remember just as accurately as they remembered when asked about words that did not appear in their confessions. But in the presence of the "truth" light, false confessions were believed: the subjects made many more errors of recall and were far less sure of their memories. Interestingly, subjects were equally misled by true statements they had made in the presence of the "lie" light. The statements were true, but the conditions were those in which the subjects had learned to distrust themselves. Hence, they did not believe their statements. As in the earlier experiment, the subjects were not aware of the systematic effects of the confessions or the lights on their ability to recall their actions. This experiment, then, confirmed my hunch that the process of self-persuasion can alter a man's recall of events if he is required to utter false statements under "truth-telling" conditions.

As I told the Senate subcommittee after demonstrating and explaining this experiment, it is conceivable that elements of the experimental procedure could be inherently present during an actual interrogation. For example, the physical surroundings of any police interrogation probably already act as "truth" signals for the average citizen because he simply could not conceive of himself or any other honest citizen making untrue statements in such circumstances. As a result, he is already in a situation in which he is very likely to be affected by his own statements. Any inadvertent errors he makes in otherwise truthful testimony he is likely to accept thereafter as being true. Furthermore, a skillful interrogator can elicit inaccurate and distorted statements by using leading questions and making "helpful" hints. ("She was carrying a brown purse, wasn't she?") Eyewitnesses can also be brought to believe any initial inaccuracies in their accounts through the same process. For example, "I did see her carrying a brown purse" is exactly analogous to "I did cross out the word *tree*" in that it is subject to the same kind of distortion through self-persuasion.

There is another technique an interrogator can employ that has a parallel in the "false confession" experiment. Just as I trained the subjects to use the amber light as a "truth" signal by having them always tell the truth when it was on, so too a skillful interrogator could set up all the cues of an interrogation as "truth" signals. He could do this by first asking several questions which the suspect or eyewitness could and would answer truthfully without hesitation. Then, when the situation had thus been established as a "truth-telling" session, the interrogator would gradually shift to questions about which the individual was uncertain, questions whose answers could be manipulated with helpful hints. By following this sequence, the interrogator would maximize the possibility that the answers to his questions would exert a self-persuasive effect on the individual.

Thus, an interrogator could create "truth" signals either inadvertently or deliberately by employing techniques parallel with those used in the experiment. He could thereby produce a witness who had become confused by the interrogation itself. There is, however, an even more ironic implication of the self-persuasion analysis of the interrogation process—the role of coercion and free choice.

Let us assume the viewpoint of an outside observer who hears an individual uttering statements about his beliefs or attitudes. Just as we have learned to disregard the statements of someone who has been bribed with money, so too we are unlikely to believe the confession of a man who has been coerced into making that confession. Like a bribe, the coercion signals to us that the person is not necessarily to be believed. He appears to be confessing only to escape harsh treatment. On the other hand, if the person appears to have volunteered his confession with little or no coercion, we are likely to take his confession as truthful. Here it is the lack of coercion that acts like a "truth" signal for us. These considerations are already part of our legal procedures; forced confessions are never acceptable as evidence.

The self-perception hypothesis, then, suggests that the suspect himself responds to the same "credibility" cues that we respond to. In this case, he uses the amount of coercion as a cue in deciding whether to believe his own statements, just as the Yale students used the amount of money they had been paid in deciding whether to believe their pro-police essays and just as the subjects used the "truth" and "lie" lights in my laboratory experiments. By threatening or coercing a man we may get him to confess whatever we want, but we are not likely to change his beliefs; it is clear to him that he is confessing only to escape aversive consequences. If, however, we can get him to confess by using very subtle pressures or very little coercion, then he is more likely to believe whatever we induce him to say.

Now consider once again the Court-imposed guidelines for interrogation. The police must inform an arrested suspect that he need not make a confession, that if he chooses to do so it is entirely up to him, that he will not be punished if he refuses to do so, and so forth. You will recognize that these are exactly the conditions—conditions of apparent free choice—under which the individual will be psychologically most affected by any confession he *does* choose to make. That is, if in spite of these warnings the interrogator is able to subtly induce the individual to confess anyway, it is *that* confession, not one obtained through coercion, that is most likely to lead the suspect to believe what he has said. In such a case, the interrogator's assurances that the suspect does not have to confess actually act as "truth" signals that tell the suspect that any statements he makes are probably true because he has no other reason for making them. It may take an interrogator longer to obtain a confession if he must warn the suspect first and then use no threats or coercion of any kind; but, if he does obtain a confession under these circumstances, it seems likely that the suspect's own beliefs will have been altered in the process. It is irrelevant if a court refuses to admit the confession as evidence; the interrogation itself will have helped create a defendant who might incriminate himself in court by means of a memory made faulty by self-persuasion.

It should be clear, of course, that the self-persuasion effect is not the only factor involved; obviously the individual has other ways of knowing what the truth really is. Nevertheless, research indicates that this effect helps determine what the individual believes to be true. Also, it is important to note that the individual does not have to be induced to make a complete set of false statements. Even inadvertent inaccuracies in an otherwise truthful confession or statement are likely thereafter to be seen as true by the individual. In fact, in actual practice, I suspect this is the most common consequence of the self-persuasion effect: small errors suddenly become facts simply by being stated under "truth light" conditions.

We are thus led to a rather ironic conclusion: it appears that the less a society uses coercive tactics in interrogation, the more susceptible the person being interrogated becomes to thought control through self-persuasion. I hope, speaking now as a private citizen, that nobody will argue from this conclusion that the police should be allowed to employ coercion in order to protect suspects from self-persuasion. On the contrary, it seems to me that these research conclusions argue for even greater legal safeguards for the suspect during interrogation. (One law professor suggested in his testimony that all interrogation sessions be recorded on tamper-proof magnetic wire and made available to attorneys for the trial.) The guarantees of the Fifth Amendment are actually less crucial in the courtroom, where attorneys and other safeguards are present, than they are in the back room of the precinct station, where these safeguards are absent.[3] The protection of the Fifth Amendment is surely vitiated if it is applied only after self-incrimination has taken place or after the defendant's memory has been distorted by self-persuasion.

ATTITUDES FOLLOW BEHAVIOR

We have seen that behavior and the conditions under which it occurs are one of the major foundations of an individual's beliefs and attitudes. And, although the cognitive, emotional, and social factors also have their effect, it remains true that changing an individual's behavior is one of the ways of causing change in his beliefs and attitudes. His new behavior provides a source from which he draws a new set of inferences about what he feels and believes.

Festinger's theory of cognitive dissonance and my theory of self-perception are two recent attempts to provide a theoretical explanation of this process of attitude change. Evidence for the existence of such a process has been around for some time, however. For example, a study of a large unionized corporation revealed that a factory worker's beliefs and attitudes changed markedly if he was elected union steward or promoted to foreman (Lieberman, 1956). Workers elected to the position of union steward became more pro-union on a number of pertinent issues; workers promoted to foremen became more pro-management. These attitude changes occurred soon after the role changes, and within three years the two groups of men had developed almost diametrically opposed sets of attitudinal positions. Furthermore, when changed economic conditions required some of the foremen to resume their previous roles of rank-and-file workers, their attitudes changed appropriately and reverted to what they were formerly. Although other studies before this one had shown that roles and attitudes are often correlated (e.g., officers are more favorable toward the army than are enlisted men [Stouffer et al., 1949]), Lieberman's study was the first to confirm the cause-and-effect sequence we have discussed here, the sequence in which behavior change causes attitude change.

BLACK AMERICANS

Playing a new role not only changes one's opinions toward external issues; it also affects one's perception of himself. Indeed, it would seem very difficult to play a particular role all of one's life without "internalizing" part of it, that is, without beginning to believe part of it. The Supreme Court recognized this fact in its 1954 decision declaring that

---

[3]For an excellent discussion of some of the tricks used by interrogators, see Zimbardo (1967a, 1967b).

public school segregation was unconstitutional: "To separate [black children] from others of similar age and qualification solely because of their race," wrote Chief Justice Earl Warren in his 1954 opinion, "generates a feeling of inferiority as to their status in the community that may affect their hearts and minds in a way unlikely ever to be undone." And, indeed, research supports this claim. One of the studies cited by the Supreme Court showed that black children as young as three years reject black dolls as inferior to white dolls (Clark & Clark, 1965). In addition, there is other research (e.g., see Pettigrew, 1964) which shows that black Americans over the years have looked at their own situation and behavior, at their impotence in the face of discrimination, and have drawn negative self-images and low self-esteem from such observations. Playing the role of "Negro" in our society has led to an internalization of that role, a self-hate, on the part of many black Americans.

But the process also works in reverse. Attitudes follow behavior, and we now know that there is no better way to make any man, black or white, become militant than to get him on a picket line or in a sit-in. Research on black students in the South in the early 1960s showed that those who were most willing to initiate civil rights actions were those who had already begun to shake off the effects of the "Negro" role. Black activists were more likely to feel that their destinies were under their own control, whereas nonparticipants felt that their destinies were in the grip of forces over which they had no control (Gore & Rotter, 1963). The black community is now deliberately and self-consciously capitalizing on this process, generating new pride and self-esteem by engaging its members in activities which demonstrate—to themselves as much as to white America—that they can exert control over their own environments. The principle remains the same: Attitudes follow behavior.

In the early 1960s white Americans often claimed that civil rights demonstrations were worthless, particularly when demonstrations failed to achieve a stated objective. Thus, in 1963 60% of white Southerners and 43% of white Northerners felt that demonstrations had "hurt rather than helped the Negro cause" (Sheatsley, 1966). Similarly, young black militants today tend to minimize the importance of the civil rights activities of the early sixties. Both of these groups, however, overlook the enormous psychological importance that these demonstrations had for changing the self-perceptions of the black community—even when the objectives of the demonstrations were relatively unimportant or were not achieved. The young militants of today owe much of their militance, their new pride in being black, and their enhanced self-esteem to the activities of their older brothers and sisters in the early sixties.

WHITE AMERICANS

White Americans provide an equally dramatic example of the attitudes-follow-behavior sequence. The pattern is now fairly familiar—before a particular desegregation action, many whites are opposed; the action is taken anyway; their attitudes then become more favorable. Thus, in the early 1960s surveys repeatedly showed that Americans felt that "pushing too hard" and, more recently, civil disorders only hurt the cause of human rights. But these same surveys have also shown that in spite of the disorders—and probably *because* of the protests—attitudes toward the goals of the human rights movement among white Americans, North and South, continue to become more favorable as each year passes. This is not to say that there is not "backlash," local setbacks, antagonism over disruptive protests, and strong opposition to violence, but for a long time attitudes toward the goals of equal justice and equality have become steadily more favorable with no major reversals since at least 1942.

And, although it is sometimes difficult to unravel causes and effects, a close analysis of the data indicates that favorable attitudes toward a particular desegregation move typically follow rather than precede the move. For example, surveys made in 1956, two years after the Supreme Court decision on school segregation, showed that only 31% of the whites in communities which had begun some token school integration approved of the move. But by 1963, when the integrated areas included many additional communities where anti-integration sentiment had been much stronger, the majority of Southern whites in those communities had accepted school integration. Nationwide attitudes toward school desegregation moved from 30% favorable in 1942, to 49% in 1956, to 62% in 1963. Even in the most hard-core areas of the South, approval of school integration rose from 4% in 1956 to 28% in 1963.[4]

Surveys on other racial issues show the same kind of pattern. We have learned that many white Americans will continue to express the view that the rate of change should slow down or even that change should stop, and many whites will always oppose any new step. But we have also learned that, at the same time these attitudes of opposition toward the next step are being expressed, attitudes toward the step that has just been taken have already begun to sanction it. Finally, all surveys reveal that attitudes toward integration on the part of both black and white Americans are more favorable in those who have experienced it and least favorable in those who have had no interracial contacts (Pettigrew, 1969). And again, the cause-effect sequence most often appears to be "behavior first, then attitudes."

---

[4]Statistics in this paragraph are from Sheatsley (1966).

We can now see one of the reasons why legislation and court decisions *can* change the "hearts and minds of men," why "stateways *can* change folkways." They do so, in part, by effecting a change in behavior; then, when behavior has been changed, attitudes often follow. This is not the whole story, however, for social norms are also involved in the attitude-change process. But that is a topic for the next chapter.

Early in this book, I suggested that if you were told any one of my opinions, you could probably guess several of the others. If you were told that I support strong civil rights legislation, for example, you could probably surmise that I was a "dove" on Vietnam, that I fear fascism more than communism, that I oppose curfew restrictions on college women, and that I worry less about the size of our national debt than about the unequal distribution of our national wealth. I claimed an equal predictability for my neighbor's opinions: if you knew that he opposes open-housing laws, you could probably guess—correctly— that he also opposes firearms registration but favors stiffer penalties for marijuana use, for homosexual behavior between consenting adults, and for disrespectful action against the American flag.

Now my neighbor and I both consider ourselves to be independent-minded men who arrive at our opinions only after considering each issue on its merits. But our predictability would seem to suggest otherwise. Of course, as the earlier discussion of the cognitive foundations of beliefs and attitudes argued, that predictability *could* be construed as evidence for the clarity of our logic and the internal consistency of our belief systems. Perhaps my neighbor and I are predictable only because each of our opinions follows in tidy, logical fashion from our basic values and primitive beliefs.

Perhaps. But we are also vulnerable to another kind of predictability whose threat to our "independent-mindedness" is not so easily dismissed: predictability from our social backgrounds. Indeed, our major beliefs, attitudes, and values lose nearly all their mystery as soon as the dominant social influences in our backgrounds are revealed. In my case, for example, any alert observer of the American scene could have my opinions pretty well pegged as soon as he learns that I was raised in an equalitarian Reform Jewish home by two Democrats in a large American city; that I received a degree from Reed College (where ordinary liberals find themselves somewhat to the right of the political center); and that I am currently a behavioral scientist at a university on the West Coast. As for my neighbor, you will probably not be startled to learn that he was raised in a Midwestern Protestant home by strict, God-fearing, Republican parents; that he was treasurer of his social fraternity at the state university where he majored in business administration; and that he is executive secretary of the local Chamber of Commerce and an active member of the American Legion. In short, a catalogue of the social influences to which my neighbor and I have been exposed is practically equivalent to a catalogue of our major beliefs, values, and attitudes. So much for "independent-mindedness."

This example illustrates some of the extensive influences which our parents, friends, teachers, and colleagues can have upon our belief systems. Social influences can also be either more superficial or more profound than these. Social influences can range from the explicit attempts of a salesman to modify single, isolated, higher-order opinions to a society's ability to inculcate an entire nonconscious ideology into its citizens, to actually create the underlying premises and basic values which generate their interpretations of the world. From the superficial and isolated to the profound and pervasive: this is the range of the social influences that concern us in this chapter.

PERSUASION VIA THE MASS MEDIA

To most people the term *social influence* evokes the image of a television announcer trying to sell a product. Further, most people seem to be suspicious, wary, and skeptical of such obvious attempts to persuade. In a public opinion poll, for example, 75% of those who had an opinion believed that television commercials used untruthful arguments; and the higher the educational level of the person asked, the more likely he was to believe it (Watson, 1966, p. 295). Perhaps you believe it too. If so, you are right. Most people also seem to believe that their skepticism renders them immune to such influence. That is, they believe that persuasion loses its effectiveness when the communicator is known to be biased and to be explicitly trying to persuade. Perhaps you believe this too. If so, you are wrong. Try the following test: Which brand of headache remedy do you use? Why? Now check your answer with the following facts.

Brand A: Perhaps you use the most widely promoted brand of plain aspirin because you have heard that it is "100% pure aspirin" and that "government tests have proved that no pain reliever is stronger or more effective than Brand A." The makers of Brand A are quite right: their brand is all aspirin, and government tests did show that no pain reliever was stronger or more effective. It is also true, however, that no pain reliever in the tests was shown to be weaker or less effective than Brand A. That is, all brands were equally strong and effective. The tests, sponsored by the Federal Trade Commission and published in the *Journal of the American Medical Association* in December, 1962, compared one of the least expensive brands of plain aspirin with the four most heavily advertised headache remedies: Brand A, the best-known buffered aspirin (Brand *B*), and the two most popular "extra-strength" combination tablets (Brand *C* and Brand *D*). The study found no significant differences between any of the five brands in either speed or effectiveness in relieving pain.

In fact, of course, there is a difference among headache remedies: price! Currently Brand *A* is selling at my neighborhood drugstore for 98¢ for a 100-tablet bottle, whereas several other national and local brands are selling for 19¢ per 100 tablets. Medical consultants to Consumers Union, the world's largest non-profit consumer testing organization, continue to emphasize year after year that "you will get as good relief from common pains and fever as is available without a prescription if you buy the least expensive U.S.P. aspirin your store sells. . . . The only significant difference among brands of aspirin plain or buffered is price" (Consumers Union, 1963, pp. 13 and 11).

Brand B: Perhaps you use buffered aspirin because you have heard that it will not upset your stomach as aspirin might or because you have been persuaded by the commercials for Brand *B* (the best-known brand of buffered aspirin) that this product works "twice as fast as aspirin." But the government tests showed that there was no significant difference between plain and buffered aspirin (Brand *B*) in speed or in the incidence of stomach upset. The makers of Brand *B* do claim to have experimental and clinical evidence of more rapid absorption for their product, but many experts have long been dubious of the way these tests were conducted, and other carefully controlled tests conducted by investigators at New York Medical College and Syracuse University showed no significant difference in speed of absorption, promptness of pain relief, or safety between plain and buffered aspirin (Consumers Union, 1963, p. 15). But if you still want buffered aspirin, you can get it for about 25¢ per 100 tablets by buying a brand whose maker is not spending a fortune on national television advertising. Brand *B* at my neighborhood drugstore commands a price of $1.49 per 100 tablets.

Brands C and D: At the time of the government tests, some headache remedies, including two of those tested, combined aspirin with phenacetin and caffeine. Accordingly, these are called APC tablets. Phenacetin has about the same effectiveness as aspirin in relieving pain and depressing fever, but it is not as good for suppressing the inflammation caused by such ailments as arthritis. As for caffeine, it is not a pain reliever, and there is no reliable evidence that it enhances the effect of aspirin either (Consumers Union, 1963, p. 14). Thus, it is not surprising that the government study found APC tablets to be no more effective than plain aspirin. The study did find, however, that APC tablets upset the stomach "with significantly greater frequency than any of the other products tested." Moreover, medical journals began to report suspicions that the prolonged use of phenacetin in substantial doses might be associated with irreversible and possibly fatal damage to the kidneys (Consumers Union, 1963).

Since that time, one of the brands tested, Brand C, has replaced phenacetin with other compounds, retained the aspirin and caffeine, and raised its price—it is now $1.59 per 100 tablets at my drugstore. The other combination tablet tested in the government study, Brand D, has simply had the phenacetin removed from it, leaving it with aspirin and caffeine. But this solution to the medical problem raised a public relations problem for the makers of Brand D. They had reportedly spent $86,400,000 on a television commercial which showed three dishes of ingredients while a narrator said that Brand D contained "not one, not two, but a combination of medically proven ingredients" (Masters, 1965, p. 220). When the number of ingredients dwindled to an unimpressive two, it seemed a shame to abandon a sales pitch effective enough to have earned more money than the movie "Gone With the Wind" (Masters, 1965, p. 220). So at first the commercial kept the three dishes of ingredients, but moved them from the foreground of the television screen back into the package. After a few more months, the three dishes were deleted from the commercial but "combination of ingredients" was still heard. The next version I saw had three dotted lines and a corresponding narration informing the viewer that Brand D contains (1) the pain reliever doctors recommend most (that's aspirin, of course), (2) plus more of that pain reliever (more aspirin), (3) plus the strength of another ingredient (caffeine). Thus 2 was made to equal 3. At the time of this writing, Brand D has switched not ingredients but ailments. The commercials are now emphasizing that it contains more of the ingredient that "doctors recommend most for relief from minor arthritis pain and stiffness." Guess what that is. At my drugstore the cost of this "extra-strength" compound is $1.39 per 100 tablets.

The test is over. How did you do? Marketing statistics indicate that you probably flunked it, that you are one of the millions of Americans whose headache dollar is spent primarily for the privilege of being persuaded to spend it. And this in spite of the fact that you claim to be "suspicious, wary, and skeptical" of television commercials.

There is a moral to this example: Persuasion does not lose its effectiveness merely because the communicator is known to be biased or known to be explicitly trying to persuade. The contrary view that persuasion *does* lose its effectiveness under these circumstances is widely held, however. It is even cited in some social psychology textbooks as a "psychological principle" of persuasion, but repeated attempts to demonstrate its validity have failed, and it now appears to be just another principle of "bubbapsychology" (McGuire, 1969, pp. 182–187). That is, it is a "psychological principle" which everybody's bubba[1] knows to be true, but which is, in fact, false.

But if my aspirin example has helped expose one principle of bubbapsychology, it runs the danger of perpetuating our belief in another, namely the Orwellian view that persuasion via the mass media is highly effective in controlling our beliefs, attitudes, and behavior. Not so. It is true that television advertising can increase purchases of small, frequently replaced merchandise (NBC, 1954); that advertising can help create knowledge of and demand for a new product; and that intense national promotion can help a group of manufacturers (such as the major aspirin companies) to dominate a particular market. In addition, the mass media undoubtedly affect a few of our beliefs and attitudes indirectly. But the rest of the case for the effectiveness of persuasion via the mass media is not very impressive.

For example, after an intensive image-building campaign for the oil industry, 13% of the sample surveyed had become more favorable, but 9% had become less favorable, a net gain of only 4% (Watson, 1966, p. 260). Furthermore, a review of the presidential campaigns from 1792 to 1940 found that the majority of newspapers were as likely to have supported the loser as the winner (Mott, 1944), and more recent studies have found that those who are most exposed to presidential campaign material in the mass media seem to be least affected by it (Berelson, Lazarsfeld, & McPhee, 1954). There are many other examples like these (see McGuire, 1969).

What accounts for these persistent failures to find measurable effects of persuasion? Some people have suggested that in commercial and political advertising, the effects of one campaign may cancel out the effects of a competing campaign. Another popular explanation is that people expose themselves only to information which supports the beliefs and attitudes they already hold. It has also been suggested that persuasive effects do occur, but that they are too subtle to be detected by the studies. These and many other possibilities *may* be true, but the evidence for them is not particularly strong (McGuire, 1969). Some of them probably even belong to the realm of bubbapsychology.

It seems to me that advertising is probably more effective as a channel of information than as a mode of persuasion. As a channel of information, a promotion can make known a real and substantial advantage of a product or candidate, but it cannot salvage a product which lacks real appeal. The failure of the Ford Motor Company to sell Edsel automobiles hardly resulted from any lack of promotion in the mass media.

---

[1] *Bubba:* Yiddish for "grandmother." (Can someone named McGuire really have a bubba?)

Most of the time, however, advertising attempts to promote one of several competing products or candidates which, like aspirin brands, are objectively very similar to one another. In these circumstances, I suspect that cancellation effects do occur and that the net effect of any single campaign will be very small. Note, however, that under these circumstances a manufacturer or candidate cannot afford *not* to advertise if his competitors do. Furthermore, an edge of a few percentage points in a statewide vote often decides an election, and a selling edge of a few percent for a product in a national market represents a sizable chunk of money. And as long as there are still bright, well-informed people like you who are willing to pay $1.50 for aspirin, Madison Avenue is not about to alter its methods just because we social psychologists can show that the impact of its persuasive messages in the mass media is both vanishingly small and psychologically insignificant for an individual's larger belief system.

You may regard television advertising as an obnoxious evil, but these research findings suggest that you need not fear that the mass media are going to "brainwash" us in some Orwellian manner. This is particularly true as long as our society permits competing channels of information to operate effectively. Why, I'll bet that you are even about to change your brand of aspirin!

INTERPERSONAL INFLUENCE

Not only have studies of the mass media demonstrated that the sophisticated techniques of mass communication do not dictate our beliefs and attitudes; they have simultaneously reconfirmed a rather homey truth that even our bubbas were right about: The major influence upon people is people. Even in our technologically advanced society, there appears to be no substitute for direct personal contact.

An example of this was provided by a study of politics in Ann Arbor, Michigan (Eldersveld & Dodge, 1954). A revision of the city charter was coming up for a vote, and 63 citizens who were either opposed to or undecided about the revision were divided into three groups for purposes of the study. Each member of the first group was personally visited in an attempt to persuade him to vote for revision of the charter. Each member of the second group received four mailings of propaganda in favor of the revision. The third group was exposed only to what they may have seen or heard in the mass media. When election day came, 75% of those who had been personally contacted voted for the revision; 45% of those who had received printed matter did so; and only 19% of the control group did so. This outcome suggests that doorbell ringing for political candidates can be an effective campaign tactic.

Results like these have generated the hypothesis that any effects of the mass media on the general population normally operate through a "two-step flow of communication" (Katz, 1957). For most of the population, certain people, usually friends, family, and community contacts, serve as "opinion leaders." These people act as mediators between the mass media and the "rank and file." That is, the ideas flow from television, radio, and the printed page to opinion leaders and from them to the rest of the community.

This two-step flow was demonstrated in a survey carried out in Decatur, Illinois (Katz & Lazarsfeld, 1955). It dealt with public affairs, marketing, fashions, and moviegoing. The participants were asked to name the persons they believed to know most about each of these topics, the persons they considered to be the most trustworthy, the persons who had actually influenced them in some specific decision, and the persons with whom they most often talked over what they had learned from the mass media and other sources. The interviewers then followed up many of the names the interviewees had given them, and then even followed up some of the names given to them by the persons first named. In this way they were able to reconstruct the patterns of influence.

The results showed that personal contacts influenced opinions and buying decisions more than did the mass media, regardless of the subject matter. However, the subject matter did determine who the opinion leaders would be. In household marketing, for example, opinion leadership was concentrated among older women with large families, whereas for fashions and moviegoing the younger unmarried girls had leadership roles. Only in public affairs was there some concentration of leadership among those of higher status. In the sample, 27% were opinion leaders in a single area; 10% were leaders in two areas; and only 3% were leaders in marketing, fashion, and public affairs. The remaining 60% of the sample constituted the rank and file on all issues.

The two-step process of information flow is not confined to the general public; it also operates within professional areas. For example, the phenomenon occurs in the medical profession (Menzel & Katz, 1956). It was found that a doctor's decision to adopt a new drug soon after it is placed on the market is determined more by how much contact he has with colleagues than by his age, the medical school he attended, the income of his patients, or his reading of medical journals. In fact, about half the members of each medical clique who adopted a new drug did so within a few days of one another, and except for the "pioneer" himself, no physician adopted a new drug unless he had had direct contact with another physician who had already used it. The pioneers, or opinion leaders, were doctors who read a large number of professional journals, who attended more out-of-town professional meetings, and who maintained contact with a greater variety of medical institutions and societies. They served as the mediators in the two-step process of influence from the sources of innovation to the general population of doctors.

It would appear that direct interpersonal influence will never become obsolete no matter how sophisticated the instruments of communication become in our technologically advanced society. Just as your bubba always said: The major influence on people is people.

SOCIAL NORMS

Opinion leaders do more than transmit information to the general population. They also help create and perpetuate the social norms of the community; that is, they serve as models who demonstrate which behaviors are appropriate and which attitudes are correct. Accordingly, the process of bringing about social change in a community is often analogous to the two-step flow of information in that the opinion leaders again provide the mediating link, which in this case is a link between an external force for change and a modification of the behaviors and attitudes of the community at large. The desegregation process in the southern United States provides a striking example.

Over the years many theories have been advanced to account for the segregated racial patterns of the South and for the overt anti-Negro sentiment expressed by many Southerners. For example, the authoritarian personality theory (discussed in Chapter 3) states that some individuals are racially prejudiced for unconscious reasons, reasons which are in turn related to an authoritarian family structure. Some observers have suggested that the South might contain a higher proportion of authoritarian families and personalities than the North. But Thomas Pettigrew, a social psychologist who specializes in race relations, has long argued that Southern segregation and prejudice are sustained primarily by simple conformity to the prevailing social norms of that region (Pettigrew, 1959). There are, of course, historical, economic, sociological, and psychological causes which brought these racial norms into being, but, according to Pettigrew, it is simple conformity which is primarily responsible for their continued existence. It is important to know which theory is correct since the prescription for social change would be quite different for the two cases. If the authoritarian personality theory is correct, mass psychotherapy might be the only path to lasting social change. If the conformity hypothesis is correct, changing the social norms via the opinion leaders would be the prescribed course of action. Accordingly, Pettigrew tested the two theories.

By employing the questionnaire that was originally developed for measuring authoritarianism, Pettigrew discovered that Southerners are not more authoritarian than Northerners. Furthermore, Southerners who are prejudiced against Negroes are not necessarily prejudiced against other out-groups, as the theory of authoritarianism would require. In fact, the South, along with the Far West, is one of the least anti-Semitic regions in the United States. A sample of white adults in Louisiana was quite favorable toward Jews but at the same time quite unfavorable toward blacks (Prothro, 1952). Finally, veterans from the South (whose army experience has brought them into contact with different social norms) are considerably more tolerant of blacks than nonveterans, in spite of the fact that veterans from both North and South are more authoritarian.

Pettigrew's conformity hypothesis is further supported by his finding that individuals who would be expected to conform more closely to social norms in general also reflect more closely the local norms with regard to racial attitudes. For example, women (who have been found to be more conforming generally) are significantly more anti-Negro than men in the South but not in the North—where social norms do not sanction *overt* anti-Negro sentiment. Similarly, respondents who explicitly identify themselves as political independents in the South are more tolerant of blacks than those who consider themselves either Democrats or Republicans. Again, no such differences were found in the Northern population. Finally, in the South, where attending church is a strong social norm, those who attend church regularly are more anti-Negro than those who do not.

The conformity hypothesis clarifies why the pattern of racial practices has often defied any kind of logic. For example, in 1952 Negro and white coal miners in McDowell, West Virginia, followed a pattern of integration below the ground and almost complete segregation above the ground (Minard, 1952). In the South, Southerners who were adjusting nicely to bus and public golf course integration were opposing public school integration. And if that pattern seems logical, then consider Nashville, where citizens were accepting school integration but opposing lunch counter integration. It is true, of course, that in each of these cases, some individuals were consistent. For example, it was estimated that about 40% of the West Virginia miners behaved consistently in a tolerant or an intolerant fashion both below and above ground. But that leaves 60% who could easily accommodate to a norm dictating either segregation or integration.

All of these findings support Pettigrew's conformity theory and suggest, further, that desegregation could often be effected without much fuss if the opinion leaders, those who set the social norms for the rest of the community, could be induced to go along. This is exactly what social psychologists have advised when policy-makers have sought their advice. Thus, it is usually advised that racial desegregation be initiated across an entire factory or community simultaneously or, if that cannot be done, that the desegregation process be initiated within the ranks of the opinion leaders first (the management levels of a factory, for example, or the upper middle class of a community). This procedure would then set the norm for the rank and file. Such advice, of course, often runs contrary to the conventional wisdom: "Our white workers would resent Negroes in management positions; we will desegregate the production line first." Even more often, of course, the advice is contrary to the self-interest of opinion leaders who would prefer to remain segregated. In fact, it was the attempt to desegregate lower- and lower-middle-class schools without also desegregating the upper-middle-class schools that helped bring on the racial crises in Little Rock, Arkansas, and New Orleans. The opinion leaders discovered that they cannot always get away with a "do-as-I-say-not-as-I-do" position since it is what they do that sets the norms.

In Chapter 6, I noted that legislation and court decisions can change the "hearts and minds of men" because when behavior has been changed, the new behavior provides a source of self-observed evidence upon which new beliefs and attitudes can be built. There is a second reason why the legal enforcement of racial equality is on sound psychological grounds: such enforcement represents a push toward greater cognitive consistency with the major values of our society. Third, in contrast to liquor prohibition and the recent attempts to curb marijuana use, the enforcement of racial justice is directed at behavior which is public, not private. We are now in a position to take the fourth and final step in this argument by noting that the legal enforcement of racial equality is directed at attitudes and behaviors which are rooted primarily in acquiescence to social norms, not in unconscious Freudian dynamics. It is for all of these reasons that we now believe and advise that stateways can, indeed, change folkways.

REFERENCE GROUPS

The social norms that partially govern our behavior and attitudes do not derive only from the opinion leaders of the community at large. Nearly every group to which we belong, from our immediate families to our society as a whole, has an implicit or explicit set of beliefs, attitudes, and behaviors which are considered appropriate for its members. Any member of a group who strays from those norms risks isolation and social disapproval; in other words, groups regulate beliefs, attitudes, and behaviors through the use of social reward and punishment. There is a second, more subtle way in which groups can influence us: by providing us with the frame of reference within which we compare and evaluate our own reactions to things. That is, groups sometimes provide us with the glasses through which we look at the world. Any group which exercises either of these two kinds of influence—that is, any group to which an individual refers for comparing, judging, and deciding upon his opinions and behaviors—is said to be one of his *reference groups*.

An individual does not necessarily belong to all of his reference groups. For example, as the discussion in the previous section showed, lower-middle-class white Southerners often use the middle-class members of their communities as their reference group on racial matters. Similarly, black Americans have in the past used the frame of reference provided by white Americans in evaluating their own worth; only recently has the black community made a conscious effort to provide its members with an alternative reference group, an alternative perspective on their ethnicity.

The influence of a reference group becomes particularly apparent when some outside influence attempts to seduce an individual away from one of the group norms. In a study by Kelley and Volkart (1952), a group of Boy Scouts listened to a speech by an adult who criticized the Scouts' emphasis on camping and woodcraft. Attitude measurement before and after the speech showed that those who valued their membership in the Scouts most showed the least change in their favorable attitudes toward camping and woodcraft. A closely related study by Kelley and Woodruff (1956) demonstrated that if an individual's reference group appears to change its mind, the individual himself is likely to do so too. These investigators had a group of students at a progressive teachers college listen to a recorded speech which called for a return to classroom methods more traditional than those advocated by so-called progressive educators. The students heard the speech interrupted seven times by applause from the audience that attended the speech. Half the students had been told that the audience was composed of members of their own college group; the other half had been told that the audience was composed of local townspeople. The results showed that the students who believed the applauding audience was composed of members of their own reference group changed their opinions about progressive education in the direction advocated in the speech more than did the students who believed the applause came from "outsiders."

REFERENCE GROUPS IN CONFLICT

Life would be simple if each of us followed the lead of only one reference group. But we don't, so it isn't. Consider the Jewish executive in a large financial institution or business firm, for example. His ethnic reference group, the Jewish community, is characteristically liberal on nearly all social and political issues and is heavily Democratic. On the other hand, his business reference groups are likely to be conservative, particularly on welfare and economic issues, and predominantly Republican. When issues or candidates are to be voted upon, such an individual often finds himself subjected to considerable "cross-pressure," both from within himself and from external sources. Similarly, imagine how complicated life must be for the Jewish War Veterans' organization. Should they have supported the Supreme Court ban on prayer in the public schools as most Jewish organizations did but as most veterans' organizations did not? (They did support it.) Should they have opposed the late Dr. Martin Luther King, Jr., whose civil rights activities were supported by many Jewish organizations, when he attacked America's involvement in Vietnam? (They did oppose him.) Surely the policy meetings of this organization must be more stimulating than those of most other veterans' organizations—organizations whose policy statements could well be generated by a computer program.[2]

Jews, of course, are not the only ones who occasionally find themselves "cross-pressured" by conflicting reference groups. In the 1960 presidential election, the hardest voters to predict were the fundamentalist Protestant who was also a registered Democrat and the Roman Catholic who was also a registered Republican. Would these voters vote for the Catholic Kennedy or the Republican Nixon?

But there is one reference group clash that stands out above all others: the conflict experienced by young people between their family reference group and their college or peer reference group. The most important and extensive study of the conflict between these two influential reference groups was the Bennington study, an examination of the political attitudes of the entire population of Bennington College, a small, very liberal, women's college in Vermont. The study was conceived and executed by social psychologist Theodore M. Newcomb, who was a faculty member at Bennington at the time. The dates of the first part of the study, 1935 to 1939, are a useful reminder to those who are just now discovering the generation gap for themselves; the Bennington study can be viewed as the first serious empirical examination of this venerable phenomenon.

There are three parts to the Bennington study. First, Newcomb examined the political attitudes of Bennington women during the years 1935 to 1939 (Newcomb, 1943). Then he and several colleagues followed up a majority of these women a quarter of a century later in 1961 and

[2] I am being only partly facetious here. There is a computer program which comes very close to doing just this (Abelson & Carroll, 1965).

1964 to see if their political positions had changed since college. And finally, he and his colleagues returned to Bennington in the early 1960s to see how the norms of the institution and its student body had changed (Newcomb, Koenig, Flacks, & Warwick, 1967). The Bennington study is not only the most extensive investigation of reference groups ever undertaken, but also one of the most ambitious and important investigations of beliefs and attitudes generally. We will consider here only the first two parts of the complete project.

The liberal reputation of Bennington College is now so well known that it tends to attract students who are already liberal in outlook. In 1960, for example, a majority of the parents who sent their daughters to Bennington were affiliated with the Democratic party. But in 1935, the first year in which Bennington had a senior class, most of the women came from conservative homes—homes, it will be noted, which could afford to send daughters to an expensive college during the depression years. Thus, in contrast to the 1960s, in 1936 over two-thirds of Bennington parents were affiliated with the Republican party. The liberal atmosphere was present at Bennington during the 1930s, but it was not then one of the reasons why most of the women selected the college.

The main finding of the early study was that each class of students became increasingly liberal politically during their four years at Bennington. For example, in the 1936 presidential campaign when about 66% of the students' parents favored the Republican candidate, Landon, over the Democratic candidate, Roosevelt, Landon was supported by 62% of the Bennington freshmen, 43% of the sophomores, and only 15% of the juniors and seniors.

Interviews with the women revealed rather clearly that their increasing liberalism reflected a deliberate choice between the two competing reference groups and between the social rewards contingent upon this choice. Statements like the following were typical:

> All my life I've resented the protection of governesses and parents. At college I got away from that, or rather, I guess I should say, I changed it to wanting the intellectual approval of teachers and more advanced students. Then I found that you can't be reactionary and be intellectually respectable (Newcomb, 1943, p. 134).

> Becoming radical meant thinking for myself and, figuratively, thumbing my nose at my family. It also meant intellectual identification with the faculty and students that I most wanted to be like (p. 131).

Not all the students adopted the liberal attitudes of the college reference group, and some of the conservative students were not even particularly aware of their own relative conservatism. Often, however, remaining conservative also implied a conscious choice between reference groups:

Family against faculty has been my struggle here. . . . Every time I've tried to rebel against my family I've found out how terribly wrong I am, and I've very naturally kept to my parents' attitudes (p. 124).

I wanted to disagree with all the noisy liberals, but I was afraid that I couldn't. So I built up a wall inside me against what they said. I found I couldn't compete, so I decided to stick to my father's ideas. For at least two years I've been insulated against all college influences (p. 119).

Not surprisingly, the students who adopted the community norms were better integrated into the college. Students identified as "most absorbed in college community affairs" came almost exclusively from the most liberal students and almost never from the most conservative students. Prestige also came with liberalism: when asked whom they would nominate as "most worthy to represent Bennington College in a national convention," students tended to nominate the most liberal women. In contrast, those who remained conservative were either oblivious to the community norms or were described by faculty and other students as negativistic, resistant, or indifferent to community concerns. According to faculty and medical reports, conservatives were also more likely to be overdependent upon their parents, and fewer conservatives gave evidence of a stable personality adjustment.

My emphasis in describing the Bennington study so far has been upon the function of the college community as the kind of reference group which exercises its influence by rewarding those who adopt its norms. But, as I noted earlier, reference groups can also serve as "frame-of-reference" groups by providing their members with new perspectives of the world. The Bennington community, particularly the faculty, provided the students with a new frame of reference on issues and events, new information and perspectives on a depression-torn America and a war-threatened world. It would thus be a mistake to conclude that Bennington students adopted and maintained their liberalism simply as a means for gaining acceptance or for revolting against their parents. More "intellectually respectable" influences also played an important role.

The combined influence of the social and intellectual factors was often mentioned by the women themselves in their interviews: "It didn't take me long to see that liberal attitudes had prestige value. . . . I became liberal at first because of its prestige value; I remain so because the problems around which my liberalism centers are important.

What I want now is to be effective in solving the problems." Another student stated it this way: "I wanted to accept the liberal ideas . . . which are dominant here. But I had to make sure they were my own, and so I spent several periods working with left-wing organizations. Now I'm more critical, and what I believe is my own." And, finally: "Prestige and recognition have always meant everything to me. . . . But I've sweat blood in trying to be honest with myself, and the result is that I really know what I want my attitudes to be, and I see what their consequences will be in my own life." (See Newcomb, 1943, pp. 136–137.)

As this last comment suggests, long-term consequences are the real test of new beliefs and attitudes. Is college-induced liberalism just a passing phase or will it maintain itself when the students leave college and return to the "real world"? The second part of the study, conducted between 1961 and 1964, demonstrated that the college-induced liberalism of Bennington students did maintain itself. The majority of the Bennington graduates remained liberal. For example, in the 1960 presidential election Kennedy was supported by 60% of those who had graduated from Bennington in the late 1930s. By way of comparison, it is estimated that Kennedy was preferred by fewer than 30% of those American women who were most similar to Bennington graduates, that is, by college-educated, middle-aged, Protestant women in the northeastern United States who were in the upper 1% of the population socio-economically (Newcomb et al., 1967, p. 48). In other words, Bennington graduates were twice as likely to prefer Kennedy to Nixon as were similar women who had not attended Bennington 25 years earlier. A similar finding emerges from the 1964 presidential election, in which it is estimated that about two-thirds of the total population of "women like Bennington graduates of the late 1930s" preferred Johnson to Goldwater. Among Bennington graduates, the preference for Johnson was 90% (Newcomb et al., 1967, p. 49).

Opinions on other issues show the same pattern. For example, 62% of the Bennington graduates approved of admitting Red China to the United Nations in 1960; 85% approved of the Negro student sit-ins and picketing; and 79% favored medicare. (It should be recalled that these were *very* liberal positions in 1960.) Finally, about 60% had worked for a candidate or political organization at some time after their graduation from Bennington. The Democratic party and other parties and candidates on the left had received help from 66% of these women, whereas the Republican party and other parties and candidates on the right were helped by only 27%.

Newcomb and his colleagues suggest that the political attitudes remained stable over 25 years primarily because the women selected new reference groups—friends and husbands—after college which continued to reinforce the attitudes they left college with. This was true of conservatives too. For example, 67% of the women who were above the median in conservatism in college married men who, in 1960, preferred Nixon over Kennedy. Only 33% of the women below the median in conservatism in college were married to men who preferred Nixon (Newcomb et al., 1967, p. 61). The Bennington study thus illustrates a general principle which Newcomb has advanced for years: We often select our reference groups because they share our attitudes, and then our reference groups in turn help develop and sustain our attitudes. The relationship is circular.

Bennington is not the only college which induces political liberalism in its students. In fact, it appears that most liberal arts colleges do so to some degree. The *National Review* (1963) conducted a large-scale survey of twelve diverse colleges and universities across the country in 1961–62 and 1962–63. The colleges were selected to represent a cross section of the various kinds of educational institutions that include a liberal arts curriculum. Of all the sophomores, juniors, and seniors polled, nearly 70% reported that significant changes had taken place in their political beliefs since entering college, and two-thirds of these had changed in a direction away from their precollege thinking. In all but two of the twelve schools the change was in the liberal direction, and even at these two schools (Marquette and Brandeis), the majority of the student body is liberal. At Marquette the students are more Democratic than their parents, and at Brandeis the students come from such liberal homes (Brandeis parents are 86% Democrats, 11% Republicans) that the percentage of students available to switch from conservative to liberal is quite small to begin with. Only 7% of Brandeis students consider themselves to be conservative, and most of the 16% who moved in the conservative direction after entering college appear to have changed from the far left to the moderate left.

Of those students who indicated in the *National Review* survey that their beliefs had changed since entering college, 40% listed lectures or assigned reading in courses as the primary agent in the change; "increased thinking about political questions" was listed by 70%; and 10% cited "personal contact with faculty members" as one of the influences. The poll also tended to show a correlation between the views of the college faculty and the views of the student body. The *National Review* thus arrives at its impeccably phrased conclusion: "The influence of the liberal arts faculty, then, is apparently a paramount factor in determining the political complexion of those college students whose views were flexible when they matriculated" (p. 281).

If you are a reader of the *National Review*, you will know that there was little joy in the editorial room when these data came in. But editor

William F. Buckley, Jr., never loses his cool. The *National Review* would never say out loud that "the diabolical influence of the leftist liberal arts faculty, then, is the paramount factor in seducing the malleable minds of our finest youth." But they must have been thinking it.

GENERATION GAPS BEGIN AT HOME

In the battle between the family reference group and the college reference group, it probably now appears to you that mom and dad always lose. This is certainly the predominant outcome for the early Bennington graduates, and some evidence suggests that parents begin to lose their influence even before "leftist college professors" enter the scene. For example, in a study of Jewish adolescents, Rosen (1955) found that if parents and peers both observed the Jewish dietary laws, 83% of the adolescents also observed them and planned to continue observing them after marriage. If both parents and peers were non-observers, 88% of the adolescents were also nonobservers. When these two major reference groups disagreed, however, 74% of the adolescents followed the peer group while only 26% followed the parents.

But surface disagreements between parents and children often mask a profound continuity between the generations in their basic values. For example, student activists on college campuses are often described as the students who are most alienated from their parents. It is said that the activists are rebelling against conservative and authoritarian homes. But for most of the activists this characterization appears to be wrong. A study of student political activists and their parents in 1966 showed that while it is true that activists are more radical than their parents, their parents are decidedly more liberal than other adults of their status (Flacks, 1967). When student activists were compared to a matched group of nonactivists, it was found that only 6% of non-activists' fathers described themselves as highly liberal or socialist, whereas 60% of the activists' fathers did so. Forty percent of the non-activists' fathers described themselves as conservative; none of the activists' fathers did so. Nor were the areas of agreement between the generations confined to political matters. Both nonactivists and their parents tended to express conventional views of achievement, material success, sexual morality, and religion. On the other hand, both activists and their parents tended to value intellectual and esthetic activities, humanitarian concerns, and self-expression and to devalue personal achievement, conventional morality, and conventional religion (Flacks, 1967, p. 68).

When student activists criticize their parents, they usually do not reject parental values but voice the objection that their parents have not lived up to those values. When these students strike out against societal institutions, they usually are not acting out a rebellion against their parents but are protesting the fact that those institutions do not fulfill the humanitarian goals or implement the equalitarian forms of decision-making they have come to know in their homes.[3]

Student activists are not the only young persons whose parents have themselves planted the seeds of later conflict. For example, many middle-class parents have taught their children that decisions about one's conduct should be made on rational grounds, that logic and evidence can be brought to bear on decisions of right and wrong. But as soon as a particularly emotional subject becomes the issue, the parents themselves betray this teaching. Drug use provides an example. Most college students, having learned from their parents the value of being well informed, know much more than their parents about the effects and dangers of the various drugs. There are some good arguments and some sound reasons for taking a cautious, conservative approach to many of the mind-expanding drugs. But parents often abdicate what influence they could exercise by continuing to confuse marijuana and heroin, by employing half-truths they have picked up from the mass media, or by reasoning circularly. Pertinent to this last point is the observation that many parent-student debates over the legalization of marijuana end with the parental assertion that marijuana use is wrong because it is illegal. Much of today's generation gap is a credibility gap.

Sexual behavior is another prominent example. The misdirected attempts of parents to control the sexual conduct of their children with ominous warnings about venereal disease and pregnancy seem to have declined somewhat in recent years. But when their children challenge them to justify their stand against premarital intercourse, few parents have rational "post-pill" arguments to substitute for these earlier scare warnings. The parents' dilemma stems from the fact that they have taught their children to treat decisions about conduct as theorems— that is, as conclusions whose validity is to be demonstrated. They then become dismayed when their children persist in treating the parental judgment against premarital intercourse as if it were debatable, rather than realizing that it is supposed to be an axiom, not a theorem. This parental "cop-out" does not escape the notice of the young.

In earlier years, the young often violated the teachings of their parents in sexual matters, but they usually agreed with their parents

---

[3]These remarks do not necessarily apply to black activists, and it now appears that the more radical protests which have surfaced since 1966 contain a small number of students with very different, more authoritarian, backgrounds. Correspondingly, their style of protest is also more authoritarian.

that they were, in fact, misbehaving. Today, the young are less likely to share this perception. When coeds and their mothers were asked "How important do you think it is that a girl be a virgin when she marries?", 88% of the mothers said that it was "very important." Only 55% of their daughters agreed. "Not important," thought 13% of the coeds, but not a single mother agreed with them (Bell & Buerkle, 1961).

To many parents, these disagreements signify an enormously increased frequency of sexual intercourse among the young, increased promiscuity, a dehumanizing of the sexual act, and an absence of a moral code. To most seniors in college, they signify little change in the frequency of sexual intercourse, a decrease in promiscuity, a humanizing of the sexual act, and the emergence of a stronger moral code.

The evidence is on the side of the young. Research shows that the frequency of premarital petting or coitus took an upward jump during the 1920s and has not changed much since (Bell, 1966). The frequency of intercourse among couples going steady or engaged has risen somewhat. But that's about it. Promiscuity, sleeping around with many partners, seems to have decreased for both men and women (Smigel & Seiden, 1968), and prostitutes are complaining that they have no clients under 30.

But values have changed since the 1920s. "What was done by a female in 1925 acting as a rebel and a deviant can be done by a female in 1965 as a conformist" (Reiss, 1966, p. 126). If there has been a sexual revolution on campus in the last decade, it is less a revolution in sexual behavior than a revolution in the ethics governing that behavior. Students are in the process of developing a set of sexual ethics based not upon a premarital-postmarital distinction, but upon the quality of the interpersonal relationship between the two people involved. The values underlying sexual conduct are increasingly becoming those of openness, honesty, and equality in the interpersonal relationship. Many parents have done their best to instill these values, but not all of these parents appear to be enthusiastic about the specific consequences that flow from their success.

Thus, the belief that parents lose out in the competition between reference groups is only partially true. In our society, the home environment still appears to be the most important socializing agent, even if the parents are unable to recognize the final product. In the next section, we shall see further evidence for the profound and pervasive effect of parental influence on the belief systems of children. We shall see that the young are often far less "liberated" than they claim. The moral of this section, however, is that the generation gap begins at home. College professors deserve only part of the credit.

CASE STUDY OF A NONCONSCIOUS IDEOLOGY: TRAINING THE WOMAN TO KNOW HER PLACE

BY SANDRA L. BEM AND DARYL J. BEM[1]

We have seen what happens when an individual's reference groups conflict. Alternative ideologies are suddenly brought into his awareness, and he is forced to select explicitly his beliefs and attitudes from among the competing alternatives. But what happens when all his reference groups agree, when his religion, his family, his peers, his teachers, and the mass media all disseminate the same message? The consequence is a nonconscious ideology, a set of beliefs and attitudes which he accepts implicitly but which remains outside his awareness because alternative conceptions of the world remain unimagined. As we noted earlier, only a very unparochial and intellectual fish is aware that his environment is wet. After all, what else could it be? Such is the nature of a nonconscious ideology.

A society's ability to inculcate this kind of ideology into its citizens is the most subtle and most profound form of social influence. It is also the most difficult kind of social influence to challenge because it remains invisible. Even those who consider themselves sufficiently radical or intellectual to have rejected the basic premises of a particular societal ideology often find their belief systems unexpectedly cluttered with its remnants.

In our view, there is no ideology which better exemplifies these points than the beliefs and attitudes which most Americans hold about women. Not only do most men and women in our society hold hidden prejudices about the woman's "natural" role, but these nonconscious beliefs motivate a host of subtle practices that are dramatically effective at keeping her "in her place." Even many liberal Americans, who insist that a black skin should not uniquely qualify its owner for janitorial and domestic service, continue to assume that the possession of a uterus uniquely qualifies its owner for precisely that.

Consider, for example, the first student rebellion at Columbia University, which took place in the spring of 1968. You will recall that students from the radical left took over some administration buildings in the name of equalitarian ideals which they accused the university of flouting. Here were the most militant spokesmen one could hope to find in the cause of equalitarian ideals. But no sooner had they occupied the buildings than the male militants blandly turned to their sisters-in-arms and assigned them the task of preparing the food, while they—the menfolk—would presumably plan further strategy. The reply they re-

[1] The order of the authors' names was determined by the flip of a coin.

ceived was the reply they deserved, and the fact that domestic tasks behind the barricades were desegregated across the sex line that day is an everlasting tribute to the class consciousness of the ladies of the left.

But these coeds are not typical, for the nonconscious assumptions about woman's "natural" role are at least as prevalent among women as they are among men. Philip Goldberg (1968) demonstrated this by asking female students to rate a number of professional articles from each of six fields. The articles were collated into two equal sets of booklets, and the names of the authors were changed so that the identical article was attributed to a male author (e.g., John T. McKay) in one set of booklets and to a female author (e.g., Joan T. McKay) in the other set. Each student was asked to read the articles in her booklet and to rate them for value, competence, persuasiveness, writing style, and so forth.

As he had anticipated, Goldberg found that the same article received significantly lower ratings when it was attributed to a female author than when it was attributed to a male author. He had predicted this result for articles from professional fields generally considered the province of men, such as law and city planning, but to his surprise the female students also downgraded articles by female authors drawn from the fields of dietetics and elementary school education. In other words, these women rated the male authors as better at everything, agreeing with Aristotle that "we should regard the female nature as afflicted with a natural defectiveness." We repeated this experiment informally in our own classrooms and discovered that male students show the same implicit prejudice against female authors that Goldberg's female students showed. Such is the nature of a nonconscious ideology!

It is significant that examples like these can be drawn from the college world, for today's college generation has the least investment in perpetuating the established ways of looking at most issues, including the role of women. As we noted in our discussion of sexual conduct, today's college students have been quick to reject those attitudes of their parents which conflict explicitly with the students' major values. But as the above examples suggest, they will find it far more difficult to shed some of the more subtle aspects of a sex-role ideology which—as we shall now attempt to demonstrate—conflicts just as surely with their existential values as any of the explicit parental commands to which they have so effectively raised objection. It is thus by examining America's sex-role ideology within the framework of values held by the most aware and sensitive of today's youth that we can best illustrate the power and pervasiveness of the social influences that produce nonconscious ideologies in a society.

THE IDEOLOGY VERSUS THE VALUE OF SELF-FULFILLMENT

The dominant values of today's student culture concern personal growth, on the one hand, and interpersonal relationships, on the other.

Accordingly, one subset of these values emphasizes the importance of individuality and self-fulfillment; the other stresses openness, honesty, and equality in all human relationships.

The major corollary of the self-fulfillment value is that each human being, male or female, is to be encouraged to "do his own thing." Men and women are no longer to be stereotyped by society's definitions. If sensitivity, emotionality, and warmth are desirable human character-istics, then they are desirable for men as well as for women. (John Wayne is no longer an idol of the young, but their pop satire.) If inde-pendence, assertiveness, and serious intellectual commitment are desir-able human characteristics, then they are desirable for women as well as for men. The major prescription of this college generation is that each individual should be encouraged to discover and fulfill his own unique potential and identity, unfettered by society's presumptions.

But society's presumptions enter the scene much earlier than most people suspect, for parents begin to raise their children in accord with popular stereotypes from the very beginning. Boys are encouraged to be aggressive, competitive, and independent, whereas girls are rewarded for being passive and dependent (Barry, Bacon, & Child, 1957; Sears, Maccoby, & Levin, 1957). In one study, six-month-old infant girls were already being touched and spoken to more by their mothers than were infant boys. When they were thirteen months old, these girls were more reluctant than the boys to leave their mothers; they returned more quickly and more frequently to them; and they remained closer to them throughout the entire session. When a physical barrier was placed be-tween mother and child, the girls tended to cry and motion for help; the boys made more active attempts to get around the barrier (Gold-berg & Lewis, 1969). There is no way of knowing for sure to what extent these sex differences at the age of thirteen months can be at-tributed to the differences in the mothers' behavior at the age of six months, but it is hard to believe that the two are unconnected.

As children grow older, more explicit sex-role training is introduced. Boys are encouraged to take more of an interest in mathematics and science. Boys, not girls, are given chemistry sets and microscopes for Christmas. Moreover, all children quickly learn that mommy is proud to be a moron when it comes to mathematics and science, whereas daddy knows all about those things. When a young boy returns from school all excited over a biology class, he is almost certain to be encouraged to think of becoming a physician. A girl with similar enthusiasm is told that she might want to consider nurse's training later so she can have "an interesting job to fall back upon in case—God forbid—she ever needs to support herself." A very different kind of encouragement. And a girl who doggedly persists in her enthusiasm for science is likely to find her parents as horrified by the prospect of a permanent love affair with physics as they would be by the prospect of an interracial marriage.

These socialization practices have their effect. By the ninth grade, 25% of the boys, but only 3% of the girls, are considering careers in science and engineering. (In the Soviet Union, approximately 35% of the engineers are women.) When they apply for college, boys and girls are about equal on verbal aptitude tests, but boys score significantly higher on mathematical aptitude tests—about 60 points higher on the College Board examinations, for example (Brown, 1965, p. 162). Those who would attribute such differences to feminine hormones should know that girls improve their mathematical performance if problems are reworded so that they deal with cooking and gardening, even though the abstract reasoning required for their solutions remains the same (Milton, 1958). It would appear that both motivation and ability have been affected.

The effects in mathematics and science are only part of the story. A girl's long training in passivity and dependence appears to exact a similar toll from her overall motivation to achieve, to search for new and independent ways of doing things, and to welcome the challenge of new and unsolved problems. Psychologists have found that elementary school girls are more likely to try solving a puzzle by imitating an adult, whereas boys are more likely to search for a novel solution not provided by the adult (McDavid, 1959). Furthermore, when given the opportunity to return to puzzles a second time, girls are more likely to rework those they had already solved, whereas the boys are more likely to try puzzles they had been unable to solve previously (Crandall & Rabson, 1960). One almost expects to hear an audible sigh of relief when a woman marries and retires from the outside world of novel and unsolved problems. This, of course, is the most conspicuous outcome of all: the majority of American women become full-time homemakers.

Such are the consequences of a nonconscious ideology.

But how does all of this militate against the goal of self-fulfillment? First of all it should be clear that the value of self-fulfillment is not necessarily being violated just because some people may regard the role of homemaker as inferior to other roles. That is not the point. Rather, the point is that our society is managing to consign a large segment of its population to the role of homemaker solely on the basis of sex just as inexorably as it has in the past consigned individuals with black skin to the roles of janitor and domestic. It is not the role itself which is at issue here, but the fact that, in spite of their unique identities, the majority of America's women end up in the *same* role.

Even if this is so, however, there are several arguments which can be advanced to counter the claim that America's socialization of its women violates the value of self-fulfillment. The three most common arguments invoke respectively (1) free will, (2) biology, and (3) complementarity.

1. The freewill argument proposes that a 21-year-old woman is perfectly free to choose some other role if she cares to do so; no one is standing in her way. But this argument overlooks the fact that society, which has spent twenty years carefully marking the woman's ballot for her, has nothing to lose in the twenty-first year by pretending that she may cast it for the alternative of her choice. Society has controlled not her alternatives, but her motivation to choose any but one of those alternatives. The so-called freedom to choose is illusory and cannot be invoked when the society controls the motivation to choose.

2. The biological argument suggests that there may really be physiological differences between men and women in, say, aggressiveness or mathematical ability. Or that there may be biological factors (beyond the fact that women can become pregnant and nurse children) which uniquely dictate that women, but not men, should stay home all day and shun serious outside commitment. Maybe female hormones really are somehow responsible. One difficulty with this argument is that female hormones would have to be different in the Soviet Union, where women comprise 75% of the physicians and, as noted above, about 35% of the engineers, and where only one married woman in twenty is a full-time homemaker. Female physiology is different, and it may account for some of the psychological differences between the sexes, but most psychologists, including us, continue to believe that it is America's sex-role ideology which causes so few women to emerge from childhood with the motivation to seek out any role other than the one that society has dictated.

But even if there really were biological differences between the sexes along these lines, the biological argument would still be irrelevant. The reason can best be illustrated with an analogy.

Those who subscribe to the value of ʃ ʃulfillment would be outraged, we submit, if every black American boʲ were to be socialized to become a jazz musician on the assumption that he has a "natural" talent in that direction, and if black parents should subtly discourage their sons from other pursuits because it is "inappropriate" for black men to become physicians or physicists. But suppose that it *could* be demonstrated that black Americans, *on the average,* did possess an innate better sense of rhythm than white Americans. Would that change outrage to acquiescence? Would that argue that a *particular* black youngster should have his unique characteristics ignored from the very beginning and that he should be specifically socialized to become a musician? We don't think so. Similarly, as long as a woman's socialization does not nurture her uniqueness, but treats her only as a member of a group on the basis of some assumed *average* characteristic, she will not be prepared to realize her own potential in the way that the values of today's college students imply she should.

The irony of the biological argument is that it does not take biological differences seriously enough. That is, it fails to recognize the range of biological differences between individuals within the same group category. Thus, recent research has revealed that biological factors help determine many personality traits. For example, the personality traits of dominance and submissiveness have been found to have large inheritable components; that is, biological factors have the potential for partially determining how dominant or submissive an individual, male or female, will turn out to be. But this potential is realized more frequently in males (Gottesman, 1963). Apparently, only the males in our culture are raised with sufficient flexibility, with sufficient latitude given to their biological differences, for their "natural" or biologically determined potential to shine through. The females, it would appear, are subjected to a socialization which so ignores their unique attributes that even the effects of biology are swamped. In sum, the biological argument for continuing America's homogenization of its women gets hoist with its own petard.

3. Many people recognize that most women do end up as full-time homemakers because of their socialization and that these women exemplify the failure of our society to raise girls as unique individuals. But, they point out, the role of the homemaker is not inferior to the role of the professional man: it is complementary but equal.

This argument is usually bolstered by pointing to the joys of taking care of small children. Indeed, mothers *and* fathers find child-rearing rewarding. But the argument appears weak when one considers that the average American woman now lives to age 74 and has her last child in her late twenties; thus, by the time the woman is 33 or so, her children all have more important things to do with their daytime hours than spend them entertaining an adult woman who has nothing to do during the second half of her life-span. As for the other "joys" of homemaking, many writers (e.g., Friedan, 1963) have persuasively argued that the role of the homemaker has been glamorized far beyond its intrinsic worth. This charge becomes plausible when one considers that the average American homemaker spends the equivalent of a man's working day, 7.1 hours, in preparing meals, cleaning house, laundering, mending, shopping, and doing other household tasks. In other words, 43% of her waking time is spent in work that commands an hourly wage on the open market well below the federally set minimum wage for menial industrial work.

The point is not how little she would earn if she did these things in someone else's home, but that this use of time is virtually the same for homemakers with college degrees and for those with less than a grade school education, for women married to professional men and for women married to blue-collar workers. Talent, education, ability, interests, motivations—all are irrelevant. In our society, being female uniquely qualifies an individual for domestic work.

It is true, however, that the American homemaker has, on the average, 5.1 hours of leisure time per day, and it is here, we are told, that each woman can express her unique identity. Thus, politically interested women can join the League of Women Voters; women with humane interests can become part-time Gray Ladies; women who love music can raise money for the symphony; and so forth.

But politically interested men run for Congress. Men with humane interests become physicians or clinical psychologists; men who love music play in the symphony; and so forth. In other words, in our society a woman's unique identity most often determines only the periphery of her life rather than its central core.

Again, the important point is not that the role of homemaker is necessarily inferior, but that the woman's unique identity has been rendered irrelevant. Consider the following "predictability test." When a boy is born, it is difficult to predict what he will be doing 25 years later. We cannot say whether he will be an artist or a doctor or a college professor because he will be permitted to develop and to fulfill his own unique identity, particularly if he is white and middle-class. But if the newborn child is a girl, we can usually predict with confidence how she will be spending her time 25 years later. Her individuality doesn't have to be considered because it will be irrelevant.

The socialization of the American male has closed off certain options for him too. Men are discouraged from developing certain traits such as tenderness and sensitivity just as surely as women are discouraged from being assertive and "too bright." Young boys are encouraged to be incompetent at cooking and child care just as surely as young girls are urged to be incompetent at mathematics and science.

One of the errors of the early feminist movement in this country was that it assumed that men had all the goodies and that women could attain self-fulfillment merely by being like men. But that is hardly the utopia that today's college students envision. Rather, the logical extension of their value of self-fulfillment would require that society raise its children so that some men might emerge with the motivation, the ability, and the opportunity to stay home and raise children without bearing the stigma of being peculiar. If homemaking is as glamorous as the women's magazines portray it, then men too should have the option of becoming homemakers. Even if homemaking isn't all that glamorous, it would probably still be more fulfilling for some men than the jobs in which they now find themselves.

And if biological differences really do exist between men and women in "nurturance," in their innate motivations to care for children, then this will show up automatically in the final distribution of men and women across the various roles: relatively fewer men will choose to stay at home. The value of self-fulfillment, therefore, does not imply that there must be equality of outcome, an equal number of men and women in each role. It does imply that there should be the widest possible variation in outcome consistent with the range of individual differences among people, regardless of sex. At the very least, the value of self-fulfillment would seem to imply that the society should raise its males so that they could fulfill their own identities in activities that might be less remunerative than those being pursued by their wives without feeling that they were "living off their wives." One rarely hears it said of a woman that she is "living off her husband."

Thus, it is true that men's options are also limited by our society's sex-role ideology, but as the "predictability test" reveals, it is still the women in our society whose identities are rendered irrelevant by America's socialization practices. In 1954 the United States Supreme Court declared that a fraud and hoax lay behind the slogan "separate but equal." It is unlikely that any court will ever do the same for the more subtle motto that successfully keeps the woman in her place: "complementary but equal."

THE IDEOLOGY VERSUS THE VALUE OF INTERPERSONAL EQUALITY

The ideological rationalization that men and women hold complementary but equal positions in society appears to be a fairly recent invention. In earlier times—and in more conservative company today—it was not felt necessary to provide the ideology with an equalitarian veneer. Indeed, the basic assumptions of the ideology have frequently been stated quite explicitly. There is certainly nothing subtle or nonconscious about the moral to be drawn from what happened In the Beginning:

> In the beginning God created the heaven and the earth. . . . And God said, Let us make man in our image, after our likeness; and let them have dominion over the fish of the sea, and over the fowl of the air, and over the cattle, and over all the earth. . . . And the rib, which the Lord God had taken from man, made he a woman and brought her unto the man. . . . And the Lord God said unto the woman, What is this that thou has done? And the woman said, The serpent beguiled me, and I did eat. . . . Unto the women he [God] said, I will greatly multiply thy sorrow and thy conception; in sorrow thou shalt bring forth children; and thy desire shall be to thy husband, and he shall rule over thee. (Gen. 1, 2, 3)

> For a man . . . is the image and glory of God; but the woman is the glory of the man. For the man is not of the woman, but the woman of the man. Neither was the man created for the woman, but the woman for

the man. . . . Let your women keep silence in the churches; for it is not permitted unto them to speak, but they are commanded to be under obedience, as also saith the law. And if they will learn anything, let them ask their husbands at home; for it is a shame for women to speak in the church. (1 Cor. 11, 14)

Wives, submit yourselves unto your own husbands, as unto the Lord. For the husband is the head of the wife, even as Christ is the head of the church; and he is the savior of the body. Therefore, as the church is subject unto Christ, so let the wives be to their own husbands in everything. (Eph. 5)

Let the woman learn in silence with all subjection. But I suffer not a woman to teach, nor to usurp authority over the man, but to be in silence. For Adam was first formed, then Eve. And Adam was not deceived, but the woman, being deceived, was in the transgression. Notwithstanding, she shall be saved in childbearing, if they continue in faith and charity and holiness with sobriety. (1 Tim. 2)

And lest it be thought that only Christians have this rich heritage of ideology, consider the morning prayer of the Orthodox Jew:

Blessed art Thou, oh Lord, our God, King of the Universe, that I was not born a gentile.

Blessed art Thou, oh Lord our God, King of the Universe, that I was not born a slave.

Blessed art Thou, oh Lord our God, King of the Universe, that I was not born a woman.

Or the Koran, the sacred text of Islam:

Men are superior to women on account of the qualities in which God has given them pre-eminence.

The sex-role ideology in these passages is hardly ambiguous, and many young people are horrified to learn that such radical inequality between the sexes is advocated in the theological literature of their own religion. Because they value equalitarian relationships generally, they are quick to reject this traditional view of the male-female relationship, and an increasing number of them even plan to enter marriages very much like the following hypothetical example.

Both my wife and I earned Ph.D. degrees in our respective disciplines. I turned down a superior academic post in Oregon and accepted a slightly less desirable position in New York where my wife could obtain a part-time teaching job and do research at one of the several other colleges in the area. Although I would have preferred to live in suburb, we purchased a home near my wife's college so that she could hav᷉ ᷉n office at home where she would be when the children returned from school. Because my wife earns a good salary, she can easily afford to pay a maid to do her major household chores. My wife and I share all other tasks around the house equally. For example, she cooks the meals, but I do the laundry for her and help her with many of her other household tasks.

Without questioning the basic happiness of such a marriage or its appropriateness for many couples, we can legitimately ask if such a marriage is, in fact, an instance of the interpersonal equality so many young people claim to value these days. Have all the hidden assumptions about the woman's "natural" role really been eliminated? Has the traditional ideology really been exorcised? There is a very simple test. If the marriage is truly equalitarian, then its description should retain the same flavor and tone even if the roles of the husband and wife were to be reversed:

Both my husband and I earned Ph.D. degrees in our respective disciplines. I turned down a superior academic post in Oregon and accepted a slightly less desirable position in New York where my husband could obtain a part-time teaching job and do research at one of the several other colleges in the area. Although I would have preferred to live in a suburb, we purchased a home near my husband's college so that he could have an office at home where he would be when the children returned from school. Because my husband earns a good salary, he can easily afford to pay a maid to do his major household chores. My husband and I share all other tasks around the house equally. For example, he cooks the meals, but I do the laundry for him and help him with many of his other household tasks.

It seems unlikely that many men or women in our society would mistake this marriage as either equalitarian or desirable, and thus it becomes apparent that the ideology about the woman's "natural" role nonconsciously permeates the entire fabric of such marriages. The point here is not that such marriages are bad or that their basic assumptions of inequality produce unhappy, frustrated women. Quite the contrary. It is the very happiness of the wives in such marriages that reveals society's success in socializing its women. It is a measure of the distance our society must yet traverse toward the goals of self-fulfillment and interpersonal equality that such marriages are widely characterized as utopian and fully equalitarian. It is a mark of how well the woman has been kept in her place that the husband in such a marriage is often idolized by women, including his wife, for permitting her to squeeze a career into the interstices of their marriage so long as his own career is not unduly inconvenienced. Thus is the white man blessed for exercising his power benignly while his "natural" right to that power remains forever unquestioned.

Such is the subtlety of a nonconscious ideology!

The existential values of today's young people would seem to require marriages in which the careers or outside commitments of both partners carry equal weight when important decisions are to be made and in which the division of labor satisfies what might be called a "roommate test." That is, the labor is divided just as it is when two men or two women room together in college or set up a bachelor apartment together. Errands and domestic chores are assigned by preference, agreement, flipping a coin, given to hired help, or—as is frequently the case—left undone.

It is significant that today's young people, many of whom live this way prior to marriage, seem to find that this kind of arrangement within marriage is foreign to their thinking. Consider an analogy. Suppose that a white male college student decided to room or set up a bachelor apartment with a black male friend. Surely the typical white student would not blithely assume that his black roommate was to handle all the domestic chores. Nor would his conscience allow him to do so even in the unlikely event that his roommate would say, "No, that's okay. I don't mind the domestic chores. In fact, I'd be happy to do them." We suspect that the typical white student would still not be comfortable if he took advantage of this offer, if he took advantage of the fact that his roommate had been socialized to be "happy" with such an arrangement. But change this hypothetical black roommate to a female marriage partner and somehow the student's conscience goes to sleep. At most it is quickly tranquilized by the thought that "she is happiest when she is ironing for her loved one." Such is the power of a nonconscious ideology.

Of course, it may well be that she *is* happiest when she is ironing for her loved one.

Such, indeed, is the power of a nonconscious ideology!

REFERENCES

Abelson, R. P. Modes of resolution of belief dilemmas. *Journal of Conflict Resolution*, 1959, **3**, 343–352.

Abelson, R. P. Computers, polls, and public opinion—some puzzles and paradoxes. *Transaction*, September 1968, **5**, 20–27.

Abelson, R. P., Aronson, E., McGuire, W. J., Newcomb, T. M., Rosenberg, M. J., & Tannenbaum, P. H. (Eds.) *Theories of cognitive consistency: A sourcebook.* Chicago: Rand McNally, 1968.

Abelson, R. P., & Carroll, J. D. Computer simulation of individual belief systems. *American Behavioral Scientist*, 1965, **8**, 24–30.

Abelson, R. P., & Rosenberg, M. J. Symbolic psycho-logic: A model of attitudinal cognition. *Behavioral Science*, 1958, **3**, 1–13.

Adorno, T. W., Frenkel-Brunswik, E., Levinson, D. J., & Sanford, R. N. *The authoritarian personality.* New York: Harper, 1950.

Allport, G. W. *The nature of prejudice.* Cambridge, Mass.: Addison-Wesley, 1954.

Bandler, R. J., Madaras, G. R., & Bem, D. J. Self-observation as a source of pain perception. *Journal of Personality and Social Psychology*, 1968, **9**, 205–209.

Barry, H., III, Bacon, M. K., & Child, I. L. A cross-cultural survey of some sex differences in socialization. *Journal of Abnormal and Social Psychology*, 1957, **55**, 327–332.

Bell, R. R. Parent-child conflict in sexual values. *Journal of Social Issues*, 1966, **22**, 34–44.

Bell, R. R., & Buerkle, J. V. Mother-daughter attitudes to premarital sexual behavior. *Marriage and Family Living*, 1961, **23**, 390–392.

Bem, D. J. An experimental analysis of self-persuasion. *Journal of Experimental Social Psychology*, 1965, **1**, 199–218.

Bem, D. J. Inducing belief in false confessions. *Journal of Personality and Social Psychology*, 1966, **3**, 707–710.(a)

Bem, D. J. Testimony before the Senate subcommittee on constitutional amendments of the Committee on the Judiciary: Hearings on criminal investigation. July 20, 1966.(b)

Bem, D. J. Reply to Judson Mills. *Psychological Review*, 1967, **74**, 536–537.(a)

Bem, D. J. Self-perception: An alternative interpretation of cognitive dissonance phenomena. *Psychological Review*, 1967, **74**, 183–200.(b)

Bem, D. J. The epistemological status of interpersonal simulations: A reply to Jones, Linder, Kiesler, Zanna, and Brehm. *Journal of Experimental Social Psychology*, 1968, **4**, 270–274.

Bem, D. J., & McConnell, H. K. Testing the self-perception explanation of dissonance phenomena: On the salience of premanipulation attitudes. *Journal of Personality and Social Psychology*, 1970, in press.

Berelson, B., Lazarsfeld, P. F., & McPhee, W. N. *Voting: A study of opinion formation in a presidential campaign*. Chicago: Univ. of Chicago Press, 1954.

Blum, G. S. *Psychodynamics: The science of unconscious mental forces*. Belmont, Calif.: Brooks/Cole, 1966.

Breger, L., & McGaugh, J. L. Critique and reformulation of "learning-theory" approaches to psychotherapy and neurosis. *Psychological Bulletin*, 1965, **63**, 338–358.

Breger, L., & McGaugh, J. L. Learning theory and behavior therapy. *Psychological Bulletin*, 1966, **65**, 170–173.

Brehm, J. W., & Cohen, A. R. *Explorations in cognitive dissonance*. New York: Wiley, 1962.

Brown, R. *Social psychology*. New York: Free Press, 1965.

Chapanis, N. P., & Chapanis, A. Cognitive dissonance: Five years later. *Psychological Bulletin*, 1964, **61**, 1–22.

Christie, R., & Jahoda, M. (Eds.) *Studies in the scope and method of "The authoritarian personality."* New York: Free Press, 1954.

Clark, K. B., & Clark, M. P. Racial identification and preference in Negro children. In H. Proshansky & B. Seidenberg (Eds.), *Basic studies in social psychology*. New York: Holt, 1965. Pp. 308–317.

Consumers Union. *The medicine show*. (Rev. ed.) Mount Vernon, New York: Consumers Union of U. S., Inc., 1963.

Cooper, J. B. Emotion in prejudice. *Science*, 1959, **130**, 314–318.

Couch, A., & Keniston, K. Yeasayers and naysayers: Agreeing response set as a personality variable. *Journal of Abnormal and Social Psychology*, 1960, **60**, 151–174.

Crandall, V. J., & Rabson, A. Children's repetition choices in an intellectual achievement situation following success and failure. *Journal of Genetic Psychology*, 1960, **97**, 161–168.

Dabney, V. The violence at Little Rock. *Richmond Times-Dispatch*, September 24, 1957, **105**, 14.

Eldersveld, S. J., & Dodge, R. W. Personal contact or mail propaganda? An experiment in voting turnout and attitude change. In D. Katz, D. Cartwright, S. Eldersveld, & A. McClung Lee (Eds.), *Public opinion and propaganda*. New York: Dryden Press, 1954. Pp. 532–542.

Elms, A. C. Role playing, incentive, and dissonance. *Psychological Bulletin*, 1967, **68**, 132–148.

Festinger, L. *A theory of cognitive dissonance*. Evanston, Ill.: Row-Peterson, 1957.

Fichter, J. *America's forgotten priests: What are they saying?* New York: Harper, 1968.

Fishbein, M. An investigation of the relationships between beliefs about an object and the attitude toward that object. *Human Relations*, 1963, **16**, 233–240.

Flacks, R. The liberated generation: An exploration of the roots of student protest. *Journal of Social Issues*, 1967, **23**, 52–75.

Free, L. A., & Cantril, H. *The political beliefs of Americans.* New Brunswick, N. J.: Rutgers Univ. Press, 1967.

Friedan, B. *The feminine mystique.* New York: Norton, 1963.

Fromm, E. *The heart of man.* New York: Harper, 1964.

Glock, C. Y., & Stark, R. *Christian belief and anti-semitism.* New York: Harper, 1966.

Goldberg, P. Are women prejudiced against women? *Transaction*, April 1968, **5**, 28–30.

Goldberg, S., & Lewis, M. Play behavior in the year-old infant: Early sex differences. *Child Development*, 1969, **40**, 21–31.

Goldman, R., Jaffa, M., & Schachter, S. Yom Kippur, Air France, dormitory food, and the eating behavior of obese and normal persons. *Journal of Personality and Social Psychology*, 1968, **10**, 117–123.

Gore, P. M., & Rotter, J. B. A personality correlate of social action. *Journal of Personality*, 1963, **31**, 58–64.

Gottesman, I. I. Heritability of personality: A demonstration. *Psychological Monographs*, 1963, **77** (Whole No. 572).

Hadden, J. K. *A house divided.* Garden City, New York: Doubleday, 1969.

Hess, E. H., Seltzer, A. L., & Shlien, J. M. Pupil response of hetero- and homosexual males to pictures of men and women: A pilot study. *Journal of Abnormal Psychology*, 1965, **70**, 165–168.

Hovland, C. I. The generalization of conditioned responses: I. The sensory generalization of conditioned responses with varying frequencies of tone. *Journal of General Psychology*, 1937, **17**, 125–148.

Janis, I. L., & Gilmore, J. B. The influence of incentive conditions on the success of role playing in modifying attitudes. *Journal of Personality and Social Psychology*, 1965, **1**, 17–27.

Jones, E. E., & Gerard, H. B. *Foundations of social psychology.* New York: Wiley, 1967.

Jones, R. A., Linder, D. E., Kiesler, C. A., Zanna, M., & Brehm, J. W. Internal states or external stimuli: Observers' attitude judgments and the dissonance theory–self-persuasion controversy. *Journal of Experimental Social Psychology*, 1968, **4**, 247–269.

Katz, E. The two-step flow of communication: An up-to-date report on a hypothesis. *Public Opinion Quarterly*, 1957, **21**, 61–78.

Katz, E., & Lazarsfeld, P. F. *Personal influence.* Glencoe, Ill.: Free Press, 1955.

Kelley, H. H., & Volkart, E. H. The resistance to change of group-anchored attitudes. *American Sociological Review,* 1952, **17,** 453–465.

Kelley, H. H., & Woodruff, C. L. Members' reactions to apparent group approval of a counternorm communication. *Journal of Abnormal and Social Psychology,* 1956, **52,** 67–74.

Kiesler, C. A., Nisbett, R. E., & Zanna, M. P. On inferring one's beliefs from one's behavior. *Journal of Personality and Social Psychology,* 1969, **4,** 321–327.

Lieberman, S. The effects of changes in roles on the attitudes of role occupants. *Human Relations,* 1956, **9,** 385–402.

Maccoby, M. Polling emotional attitudes in relation to political choices. Unpublished paper, 1968.

Marx, G. T. *Protest and prejudice: A study of belief in the black community.* New York: Harper, 1967.

Masters, D. *The intelligent buyer's guide to sellers.* Mount Vernon, New York: Consumers Union, 1965.

McClintock, C. G., Spaulding, C. B., & Turner, H. A. Political orientations of academically affiliated psychologists. *American Psychologist,* 1965, **20,** 211–221.

McDavid, J. W. Imitative behavior in preschool children. *Psychological Monographs,* 1959, **73** (Whole No. 486).

McGuire, W. J. A syllogistic analysis of cognitive relationships. In C. I. Hovland & M. J. Rosenberg (Eds.), *Attitude organization and change.* New Haven, Conn.: Yale Univ. Press, 1960. Pp. 65–111.

McGuire, W. J. The current status of cognitive consistency theories. In S. Feldman (Ed.), *Cognitive consistency: Motivational antecedents and behavioral consequences.* New York: Academic Press, 1966. Pp. 1–46.

McGuire, W. J. The nature of attitudes and attitude change. In G. Lindzey & E. Aronson (Eds.), *The handbook of social psychology.* (2nd ed.) Vol. 3. Reading, Mass.: Addison-Wesley, 1969. Pp. 136–314.

Menzel, H., & Katz, E. Social relations and innovations in the medical profession: The epidemiology of a new drug. *Public Opinion Quarterly,* 1956, **19,** 337–352.

Menzies, R. Conditioned vasomotor responses in human subjects. *Journal of Psychology,* 1937, **4,** 75–120.

Mills, J. Comment on Bem's "Self-perception: An alternative interpretation of cognitive dissonance phenomena." *Psychological Review,* 1967, **74,** 535.

Milton, G. A. Five studies of the relation between sex role identification and achievement in problem-solving. Technical Report No. 3, Yale University, December 1958.

Minard, R. D. Race relations in the Pocahontas coal field. *Journal of Social Issues,* 1952, **8,** 29–44.

Mott, F. L. Newspapers in presidential campaigns. *Public Opinion Quarterly,* 1944, **8,** 348–367.

National Broadcasting Company. *Why sales come in curves.* New York: N. B. C., 1954.

National Review. A survey of the political and religious attitudes of American college students. October 8, 1963, 279–302.

Newcomb, T. M. *Personality and social change.* New York: Dryden Press, 1943.

Newcomb, T. M., Koenig, K. E., Flacks, R., & Warwick, D. P. *Persistence and change: Bennington College and its students after twenty-five years.* New York: Wiley, 1967.

Peak, H. Attitude and motivation. In M. R. Jones (Ed.), *Nebraska symposium on motivation.* Lincoln, Neb.: Univ. of Nebraska Press, 1955. Pp. 149–188.

Pettigrew, T. F. Regional differences in anti-Negro prejudice. *Journal of Abnormal and Social Psychology,* 1959, **59,** 28–36.

Pettigrew, T. F. Social psychology and desegregation research. *American Psychologist,* 1961, **16,** 105–112.

Pettigrew, T. F. *A profile of the Negro American.* Princeton, N. J.: Van Nostrand, 1964.

Pettigrew, T. F. Racially separate or together? *Journal of Social Issues,* 1969, **25,** 43–69.

Piliavin, J. A., Piliavin, I. M., Loewenton, E. P., McCauley, C., & Hammond, P. On observers' reproductions of dissonance effects: The right answers for the wrong reasons? *Journal of Personality and Social Psychology,* 1969, in press.

Porier, G. W., & Lott, A. J. Galvanic skin responses and prejudice. *Journal of Personality and Social Psychology,* 1967, **5,** 253–259.

Prothro, E. T. Ethnocentrism and anti-Negro attitudes in the deep South. *Journal of Abnormal and Social Psychology,* 1952, **47,** 105–108.

Rachman, S., & Eysenck, H. J. Reply to a "critique and reformulation" of behavior therapy. *Psychological Bulletin,* 1966, **65,** 165–169.

Reiss, I. L. The sexual renaissance: A summary and analysis. *Journal of Social Issues,* 1966, **22,** 123–137.

Roessler, R. L., & Brogden, W. J. Conditioned differentiation of vasoconstriction to subvocal stimuli. *American Journal of Psychology,* 1943, **56,** 78–86.

Rokeach, M. *The open and closed mind.* New York: Basic Books, 1960.

Rokeach, M. *Beliefs, attitudes, and values.* San Francisco: Jossey-Bass, 1968.

Rosen, B. C. Conflicting group membership: A study of parent-peer group cross pressures. *American Sociological Review,* 1955, **20,** 155–161.

Rosenberg, M. J. Cognitive structure and attitudinal affect. *Journal of Abnormal and Social Psychology,* 1956, **53,** 367–372.

Rosenberg, M. J. An analysis of affective-cognitive consistency. In C. I. Hovland & M. J. Rosenberg (Eds.), *Attitude organization and change.* New Haven, Conn.: Yale Univ. Press, 1960. Pp. 15–64.

Rosenberg, M. J. When dissonance fails: On eliminating evaluation apprehension from attitude measurement. *Journal of Personality and Social Psychology*, 1965, **1**, 28–42.

Sarnoff, I. Psychoanalytic theory and social attitudes. *Public Opinion Quarterly*, 1960, **24**, 251–279.

Schachter, S. Obesity and eating. *Science*, 1968, **161**, 751–756.

Schachter, S., & Gross, L. P. Manipulated time and eating behavior. *Journal of Personality and Social Psychology*, 1968, **10**, 98–106.

Schachter, S., & Singer, J. Cognitive, social, and physiological determinants of emotional state. *Psychological Review*, 1962, **69**, 379–399.

Sears, R. R., Maccoby, E. E., & Levin, H. *Patterns of child rearing.* Evanston, Ill.: Row-Peterson, 1957.

Sheatsley, P. B. White attitudes toward the Negro. *Daedalus*, 1966, **95**, 217–238.

Smigel, E. O., & Seiden, R. The decline and fall of the double standard. *The Annals of the American Academy of Political and Social Science*, 1968, **376**, 6–17.

Staats, A. W., & Staats, C. K. Attitudes established by classical conditioning. *Journal of Abnormal and Social Psychology*, 1958, **57**, 37–40.

Stark, R., & Glock, C. Y. *American piety: The nature of religious commitment.* Berkeley and Los Angeles: Univ. of California Press, 1968.

Stark, R., & Glock, C. Y. *By their fruits: The consequences of religious commitment.* Berkeley and Los Angeles: Univ. of California Press, 1969.

Stouffer, S. A., Suchman, E. A., DeVinney, L. C., Star, S. A., & Williams, R. M., Jr. *Studies in social psychology in World War II. Vol. 1. The American soldier: Adjustment during army life.* Princeton, N. J.: Princeton Univ. Press, 1949.

Valins, S. Cognitive effects of false heart-rate feedback. *Journal of Personality and Social Psychology*, 1966, **4**, 400–408.

Volkova, V. D. On certain characteristics of conditioned reflexes to speech stimuli in children. *Fiziologicheskii Zhurnal SSSR*, 1953, **39**, 540–548.

Walker, E. L. *Conditioning and instrumental learning.* Belmont, Calif.: Brooks/Cole, 1967.

Watson, G. *Social psychology: Issues and insights.* New York: Lippincott, 1966.

Zajonc, R. B. Cognitive structure and cognitive tuning. Unpublished doctoral dissertation, University of Michigan, 1954.

Zimbardo, P. G. The psychology of police confessions. *Psychology Today*, June 1967, **1**, 16. (a)

Zimbardo, P. G. Toward a more perfect justice. *Psychology Today*, July 1967, **1**, 44–46. (b)

NAME INDEX

Abelson, R. P., 2, 28, 34, 35, 38, 39, 81, 100
Adorno, T. W., 22, 100
Allport, G. W., 9, 100
Anderson, B. F., vii
Aristotle, 90
Aronson, E., 34, 100, 103
Bacon, M. K., 91, 100
Bandler, R. J., 57, 100
Barry, H., III, 91, 100
Bell, R. R., 88, 100
Bem, D. J., iii, 56, 57, 59, 60, 62, 89, 100, 101
Bem, S. L., iv, viii, 89
Berelson, B., 74, 101
Blum, G. S., 23, 101
Breger, L., 47, 101
Brehm, J. W., 55, 56, 101, 102
Brogden, W. J., 42, 104
Brown, R., 92, 101
Buckley, William F., Jr., 86
Buerkle, J. V., 88, 100
Cantril, H., 35, 36, 37, 38, 102
Capote, Truman, 62
Carroll, J. D., 81, 100
Cartwright, D., 101
Chapanis, A., 56, 101
Chapanis, N. P., 56, 101
Child, I. L., 91, 100
Christie, R., 23, 101
Clark, E. V., vii
Clark, H. H., vii
Clark, K. B., 67, 101
Clark, M. P., 67, 101
Cohen, A. R., 55, 56, 59, 101
Cooper, J. B., 41, 101
Couch, A., 38, 101
Crandall, V. J., 92, 101
Dabney, V., 1, 101
DeVinney, L. C., 105
Dodge, R. W., 75, 101
Eldersveld, S. J., 75, 101
Elms, A. C., 56, 101
Eysenck, H. J., 47, 104

Feldman, S., 103
Festinger, L., 54, 56, 66, 101
Fichter, J., 30, 102
Fishbein, M., 25, 102
Flacks, R., 82, 86, 102, 104
Free, L. A., 35, 36, 37, 38, 102
Frenkel-Brunswik, E., 22, 100
Freud, Sigmund, 21
Friedan, B., 94, 102
Fromm, E., 18, 19, 20, 21, 102
Gerard, H. B., 10, 102
Gilmore, J. B., 60, 102
Glock, C. Y., 30, 31, 32, 102, 105
Goldberg, P., 90, 102
Goldberg, S., 91, 102
Goldman, R., 52, 102
Goldwater, Barry, 18, 19, 36, 37, 40, 53, 84
Gore, P. M., 67, 102
Gottesman, I. I., 94, 102
Gross, L. P., 52, 105
Hadden, J. K., 29, 30, 102
Hammond, P., 56, 104
Hendrix, C. T., viii
Hess, E. H., 40, 102
Hitler, Adolph, 18, 19
Hovland, C. I., 43, 102, 103, 104
Humphrey, Hubert H., 20
Jaffa, M., 52, 102
Jahoda, M., 23, 101
Janis, I. L., 60, 102
Johnson, Lyndon B., 19, 84
Jones, E. E., 10, 102
Jones, M. R., 104
Jones, R. A., 56, 102
Katz, D., 101
Katz, E., 76, 102, 103
Kelley, H. H., 80, 103
Keniston, K., 38, 101
Kennedy, John F., 81, 84, 85
Kennedy, Robert F., 20, 21
Kiesler, C. A., 56, 102, 103
King, Martin Luther, Jr., 32, 81
Koenig, K. E., 82, 104

SUBJECT INDEX